COMBAT MANUAL
Prayer Counseling For Deliverance

LAUREL T. HUGHES, Ph.D.

Word Vision Ministries, Inc.
1988

Unless otherwise indicated, all Scripture references are from the HOLY BIBLE, NEW INTERNATIONAL VERSION Copyright ©1973, 1978, 1984. International Bible Society. Used by permission of Zondervan Bible Publishers.

Printed in the United States of America.
Published by Word Vision Ministries Incorporated
Maitland, Florida USA 32751-7621.

Library of Congress Catalog Card Number: 88-51615

Library of Congress Cataloging-in-Publication Data
Hughes, Laurel Tarris
   Combat manual- prayer counseling for deliverance/Laurel T.
   Hughes, PhD.
      p. cm.
   Bibliography: þ
   ISBN 0-926392-00-X (pbk.)
   1. Bible Reference. 2. Devil and Demonology. 3. Prayer
I. Title. II. Author. III. Subject.
1988.

Cover design and artwork were skillfully and prayerfully done by Andrew Davenport of Winter Springs, Florida.

Word Vision Ministries books are available at special discounts for bulk purchase for educational seminars or group use. For details please contact:

Education Director
Word Vision Ministries Inc.
P. O. Box ~~7621~~ 941353
Maitland, Florida 32751-~~7621~~
United States of America

"He has made all things beautiful in His time."
Ecclesiastes 3:11

This book is adoringly dedicated to the "Presence of the Lord" who is my constant and consistent Holy Companion, Mentor, Guide, Teacher, Friend, the Rock of all Ages: my Precious Life.

Very special love and appreciation is given to Alton and Genevieve Tarris who have each provided immeasurable, life-long guidance and spiritual fellowship. Thank you, God, for such perfect and wonderful parents.

May I also add a prayer-filled dedication for all those who are determined to allow the Lord God access to their spirits by the revelations found in these pages. They are those who, at all personal costs, desire the Lordship and light of Christ to penetrate their most secret recesses where He alone can cleanse, fill, and empower for health and service. You, friend, will receive, because you are no longer afraid to give yourself away. You, I pray, will be totally covered by the precious protection that Christ's blood-sacrifice provides as you come into liberty, grow strong, and help lead others into truth and wholeness.

Laurel T. Hughes, PhD
New Smyrna Beach, Florida
26 June 1988

Contents

Contents

Please tell me of your deliverance experiences. Send all correspondence with a stamped, self-addressed envelope (if you want a reply) to:

WORD VISION MINISTRIES INC.
Post Office Box ~~1621~~ 941353
Maitland, Florida 32751-~~7534~~
United States of America

Prelude

COMBAT MANUAL—Prayer Counseling For Deliverance was written as a practical guide to those called into the ministry of deliverance from demonic oppression. It addresses the mature Christian, deliberately speaking to those who are victoriously walking with the Lord in spiritual strength to help others along the path of life. Prayer counselors will appreciate its instructional format and ease of finding appropriate scriptures.

For those who feel God is leading you in the direction of this service, Chapter 10 will guide you into the inherent qualifications and responsibilities of the task. The appendices are the workmen of this book. Consider reading the Glossary of Terms (Appendix IV) before beginning the main text in order to understand what the author means when certain terms are used.

As a way of explanation in helping you understand how ***Combat Manual*** was written, original meanings and expanded definitions of certain key words are used and presented in Hebrew (Old Testament) and in Greek (New Testament). So very much has been lost or hidden in the translation process that this method will prove useful in realizing the scope of deliverance with its full blessings of truth that God wishes for His people.

Another note deserving attention deals with the use of names in this book. Names are extremely important and powerful. God has particular names for each of His children written in the Book of Life. There is power in a name and what it represents. Jesus Christ is the most powerful Name existent because of the perfect blood sacrifice He made that totally met all Father-God's standards. And because we are His children and servants of righteousness, He has given His authority to us to minister salvation, healing, and exorcism in that Name. Indeed, we are commanded to do so as we go out in His name (Mark 16:15-18).

It has been an extraordinary experience for me to learn, practice, and then write down this one small corner of Truth. Take from the banqueting table what you need. Leave for others what does not apply to you. But what Truth is represented here as the teachings of Jesus Christ—you will know, and it will set you free (John 8:32).

God's blessings be on those who seek to serve Him in liberating the captives. And special blessings on those who encouraged me in the work.

Laurel T. Hughes

Chapter 1

The Purpose Of The Deliverance Ministry

The Ministry Of Intercession

The purpose of intercessory prayer for the deliverance of God's people from Satanic influence is one of God's most grace-filled provisions. This intercession ministry enables His people to move into and maintain the fullness of their salvation with purity and holiness.

Deliverance is a cleansing experience for every Christian who has wandered from or chosen paths that are contrary to the Holy Spirit's gentle guidance. It is for those who are struggling against oppressing odds, who cannot gain victory over their carnal desires, who continue to love the world and are the brunt of Satan's attacks. This is God's continuing way of renewal and escape from the snare of the fowler.

The ministry of deliverance through standing in the spiritual gap by intercession, is a calling of Christ that uses the specifics of the fruit and gifts of the Holy Spirit. It is a helping ministry enabling the overcomed to become overcomers. The ministry, so engaged, is given on behalf of overcomed believers willing to allow Jesus Christ full lordship of their lives. It demands a new commitment to being filled and controlled only by the Spirit of God and by no other spirits.

It should be kept in mind that this book as a deliverance manual was written especially for those who are called into this ministry. It is written for Christians as a guide in spiritual warfare for the spiritually mature. However, others who are not engaged in ministry can gain knowledge from its reading and be able to use it for personal application.

If you are not a part of a church fellowship engaged in this ministry where you can find help or have other specific questions that are unanswered after reading this manual, you may write to the author at the Word Vision Ministries address for assistance.

Chapter 1

What Is The Basis Of Spiritual Problems?

Christians have asked me, "Where do all my problems come from? No matter what I do to follow God, strange things happen to divert me from being on top. It seems I just get further into debt or the children get sick, or something happens in my business that is totally unforeseen. I just can't figure out what is wrong!"

This is a good beginning question. Its answer lies in tracing the problem root to one or more of the following reasons why believers are plagued by demonic influence, cursed living, or family disaster. Many spiritual problems are the result of:

1. Not knowing God's WAYS or WILL.
2. Not knowing, believing, or trusting God's CHARACTER.
3. Not allowing Jesus Christ's LORDSHIP in every area of life.
4. Not being willing to HEAR as well as OBEY the voice of God.
5. Not loving God with your whole being.

If with God's promised help you do not overcome the temptations of life, the sins of your self-nature, or the wiles of the devil, you will be overcome by whatever you fail to overcome. To whatever you give the pre-eminence and priority to, will be the exact thing that will dominate your life. The positive side is to put God first, leading you into His blessings. However, if those priorities are out of God's will, they become idols that will erect a spiritual lordship within your spirit gradually allowing Satan access to steal your freedom in Christ.

Any problem a Christian cannot overcome by either prayer and fasting, repentance and forgiveness, the avid study of God's Word, or by spiritual discipline, is most likely due to an outside hindering force not natural to them. These characteristics show an evil spirit(s) in operation which is allowed power through the setting up of personal idols.

Demonic spirits deceive believers by placing within them unbelief that robs faith for prayer. Thus, deception will spiritually blind them to the true cause of their problem. Spiritual, outside hindrances cause true blindness in the human spirit to see Jesus Christ as the Cure for all their ailments, problems, oppressions, possessions, lack of fleshly control, and mental disturbances. They are overcomed by unbelief.

Often this uncomfortable state escalates into anxiety or panic, causing the blinded believer to seek answers for their problems from world philosophies instead of looking to God alone. These people, now harrassed in their spirits, souls and/or bodies, may become extremely angry at God or others for "what they are going through". When these thoughts turn to unresolved bitterness and compulsive hatred, it will keep them from establishing a loving, open relationship with God in order to find true peace, meaning, and purpose to life. All this is traceable to a deceiving spirit.

Satan of course, is pleased at his own helpfulness in the disasterous, opportunity-wasted events in a believer's life and continues to ever bind and blind his victims for eventual destruction if possible. This root of bitterness will move out of a life only by repentance and deliverance. That will be outlined in more detail in Chapter 5.

There are about 1700 places in the Bible denoting 'deliver'. 'deliverance', 'deliverer', and the like. Deliverance from evil spirits removes the supernatural part of a problem; then people can deal with the natural attachment of the spirit, soul, and flesh. Here are some verses on God's provision for deliverance for those who are bound:

> *"You must actively obey Him in everything He commands. Only then will you be doing what is right and good in the Lord's eyes. If you obey Him, all will go well for you, and you will be able to go in and possess the good land which the Lord promised your ancestors. YOU WILL ALSO BE ABLE TO THROW OUT ALL THE ENEMIES LIVING IN YOUR LAND AS THE LORD AGREED TO HELP YOU."* Dt 6:17-19 (LIV).

> *"..I will give you peace, and you will go to sleep without fear. I will chase away the dangerous animals. YOU WILL CHASE YOUR ENEMIES..For I am the Lord your God who brought you out..WITH INTENTION THAT YOU BE SLAVES NO LONGER: I HAVE BROKEN YOUR CHAINS AND WILL MAKE YOU WALK WITH DIGNITY."* Lev 26:6-13 (KJV).

Other Scriptures About Deliverance: Galatians 5:1; Psalm 34:19; Exodus 14:13; Deut 28:47-48; Isaiah 59:1-2; 1 Samuel 17:47 (The Battle is the Lord's); Judges 2:2-3; Joel 2:32; John 8:49; Joshua 23:10, 24:12; 2 Cor 1:10, 3:18; Proverbs 11:21; 1 John 3:8.

The Deliverance Ministry of Jesus Christ

It is most interesting and vital to see how our Lord ministered deliverance, salvation, and healing during His short walk on earth. Notice that

Chapter 1

He healed ALL who came to Him of WHATEVER problem, no matter how strong or violent the demons were. In some places where He ministered, people's faith was stronger and He could do more. This meant that although the gift of healing within Jesus never changed or "lost power", the faith level of those with whom He worked with was subject to their own allowed level of belief. In some places, the Son of God Himself could not deliver or give healing because they simply were not ready to receive.

Yet, Jesus Christ is the all-powerful Son of God, God Himself, and a strong deliverer in the day of trouble to those who turn to Him. Let's begin with His own call to this ministry with the very prophecy He fulfilled taken from Isaiah 61.

"The Spirit of the Lord is upon me because He hath anointed me to preach the gospel to the poor; He hath sent Me to heal the broken-hearted, to preach DELIVERANCE TO THE CAPTIVES, and recovering of sight to the blind, TO SET AT LIBERTY THEM THAT ARE BRUISED." Lk 4:18 (KJV).

"And Jesus went about all Galilee teaching in their synagogues, and preaching the gospel of the kingdom, and healing all manner of sickness.." (Greek *NOSOS/NOSEO* - to have a diseased appetite, to hanker after [crave a sickness], dote upon, a malady, disability, disease, infirmity; clutching to self an evil thing)..

"..and all manner of disease.." (Greek *MALAKIAN* softness or weakness to diseases) *"..among the people. And His fame went throughout all Syria and they brought unto Him all sick [frail, impotent] people that were taken with diverse diseases [held in the custody of, or is a prisoner of physical trouble], and torments..."* (Greek *BASANISMOS/KAKOS* - to maltreat, torture, make evil affected, vex, hurt, harm, pain, toil, toss)..

"..those which were possessed with devils and those which were lunatic, and HE HEALED THEM ALL." Mt 4:23-24 (KJV).

"Now when the sun was setting, all they that had any sick with divers diseases, brought them unto Him and He laid His hands on EVERYONE OF THEM AND HEALED THEM. And DEVILS ALSO CAME OUT OF MANY, crying and saying, Thou art Christ, the Son of God. And He rebuked them suffering them not to speak: for they KNEW that He was Christ." Lk 4:40-41, Mt 8:16, Mk 1:32-33 (KJV).

"When Jesus rose early on the first day of the week, He appeared first to Mary Magdalene, OUT OF WHOM HE HAD DRIVEN SEVEN DEMONS." Mk 16:9.

"How God anointed and consecrated Jesus of Nazareth with the (Holy) Spirit and strength and ability and power; how He went about doing good and in particular CURING ALL THAT WERE HARASSED AND OPPRESSED BY (THE POWER OF) THE DEVIL, for God was with Him." Acts 10:38 (AMP).

"..Every kingdom divided against itself will be ruined, and every city or household divided against itself will not stand. If Satan drives out Satan, he is divided against himself. How then can his kingdom stand? And if I drive out demons by Beelzebub, by whom do your people drive them out? ..BUT IF I DRIVE OUT DEMONS BY THE SPIRIT OF GOD, THEN THE KINGDOM OF GOD HAS COME UPON YOU..

.."Or again, how can anyone enter a strong man's house and carry off his possessions unless he first ties up the strong man? Then, he can rob his house. He who is not with Me is against Me, and he who does not gather with Me scatters." Mt 12:25-30.

NOTE: The Holy Spirit of God is the Power for deliverance and after you are cleansed of demonic influence or vexation, the Kingdom of God which is righteousness, peace, and joy in the Holy Spirit has come upon you (Ro 14:17).

Other Scriptures: blind and dumb spirits (Matthew 12:22-24, Luke 9:14-15); epileptic spirits (Mark 9:17-29, Luke 9:37-43); unclean spirits (Mark 1:23-27, Luke 11:24-26); the children of God have deliverance (Mt 15:22-28); spirit of infirmity (Luke 13:10-13), and a legion of many devils staying a long time (Lk 8:26-32). Commissioning of the 70 disciples to cast out demons (Luke 10:1-17).

Jesus promised in John 14:12, that his followers would do the same works and even greater works than those He did. The Christians who hear His voice and follow His teachings these two thousand years after the resurrection, continue to have this same promise and commission. The baptism in the Holy Spirit with its gifts, callings, miracles, signs and wonders is for today, too! These are living and obvious ways God uses to proclaim the full Gospel to all who want to be whole right now. But first, we are going to get a close-up look at our enemy.

Chapter 2

Who Is Satan And His Hordes

The first two words we will look at are "Satan" and "devils". There is only one translation for Satan in the Hebrew which is the same word, *SATAN*. It means "to attack, accuse; the archenemy of good; to be an adversary, resister, opponent, be Satan, and withstand. In New Testament Greek, *SATANAS* means "Satan, the devil; the accuser."

The Old Testament Hebrew for devil is *SAIYR* or "shaggy, a he-goat, a fawn—devil; goat, kid, hairy, rough, Satyr". The root from which *SAIYR* comes is *SA'AR* meaning "to shiver; fear, be horribly afraid, hurl as a storm, be tempestuous, come like (take away as with) a whirlwind." The word roots of *SHED* and *SHUWD* mean "a doemon (demon) as malignant, be devil-like; to swell up (insolence), to devastate, waste."

The New Testament Greek root word for devil is *DAIMONIZOMAI*. "To be exercised by a demon, to have a (be vexed, be possessed with) devil(s); a demonic being, a diety—devil, god, devilish. *DAIMON* is a root word of *DAIO* and means "to distribute fortunes; a demon or supernatural spirit (of a bad nature), a devil."

CHRISTIANS ARE NOT POSSESSED (OWNED) BY DEMONS, BUT MAY BE POSSESSED WITH, IN THE SENSE OF CO-INHABITED WITH DEMON(S) WHO WISH TO LIVE WITHIN PEOPLE TO EXHIBIT THEIR POWER AND EVIL PERSONALITIES. DEMONS LIVE WITHIN TO ACT OUT SATAN'S KINGDOM.

It is important to realized that Satan's influence in a life is to vex, torment, devastate, waste it, and to kill. Whatever demonic influences a Christian experiences is present because permission (the right by will) to be there was given by that Christian. In God's economy, deliverance is the "exit door" by which the Christian boots Satan out and reverses that process.

In actual fact, the Christian is possessed (ownership) by the Lord Jesus Christ because He paid the price at Calvary with His own precious blood. What security we have in Him and responsibility to keep His Lordship in control!

These next verses show the prayer counselor's commission and call to action (not passivity) in deliverance for ourselves and in ministry:

"Finally, be strong in the Lord and in his mighty power. Put on the full armor of God so that you can TAKE YOUR STAND AGAINST THE DEVIL'S SCHEMES. For our struggle is not against flesh and blood, but against THE POWERS OF THIS DARK WORLD and against the SPIRITUAL FORCES OF EVIL IN THE HEAVENLY REALMS." Eph 6:10-12

"The desert and the parched land will be glad; the wilderness will rejoice and blossom...Strengthen the feeble hands, steady the knees that give way; say to those with fearful hearts, 'Be strong, do not fear; your God will come, He will come with vengeance; with divine retribution—He will come to save you.' "

..*"Then will the eyes of the blind be opened and the ears of the deaf unstopped. Then will the lame leap like a deer, and the mute tongue shout for joy. Water will gush forth in the wilderness and streams in the desert. The burning sand will become a pool, the thirsty ground bubbling springs.*

..*"In the haunts where jackals once lay, grass and reeds and papyrus will grow. And a highway will be there; it will be called THE WAY OF HOLINESS. The unclean will not journey on it; IT WILL BE FOR THOSE WHO WALK IN THAT WAY; wicked fools will not go about on it. No lion will be there, nor will any ferocious beast get up on it; they will not be found there. BUT ONLY THE REDEEMED OF THE LORD WILL WALK THERE, AND THE RANSOMED OF THE LORD WILL RETURN.*

..*"They will enter Zion with singing; everlasting joy will crown their heads. Gladness and joy will overtake them, and sorrow and sighing will flee away."* Isaiah 35:1-10.

"Everyone who has this hope in him PURIFIES HIMSELF, just as He is pure." .1 Jn 3:3.

"But just as He who called you is holy, so be holy in all you do...it is written: 'BE HOLY, BECAUSE I AM HOLY.' " 1 Pe 1:15.

"..LET US PURIFY OURSELVES FROM EVERYTHING that contaminates body and spirit, perfecting holiness out of reverence for God." 2 Cor 7:1.

"For He chose us in Him before the creation of the world TO BE HOLY AND BLAMELESS IN HIS SIGHT." Eph 1:4.

Moving Into Deliverance

The New Testament exorcism of devils by Jesus and His disciples before the Cross-death of Christ, established the divine authority He submitted to that clearly marked Him as Jehovah God's Son. He was not equal with others in His day who had some limited ability in using evil sources of power to cast out or subdue demons. These were the sorcerers and seers who made a living at it. No, the hallmark of Christ's ministry was the total deliverance each and every time of ALL who came to Him. His Source was divine and permanent.

Christ's ministry never failed. Every word He spoke was sent to do a job and did it consistently. Deliverance was used as a tool for healing people and pointing them toward the Calvary experience to come. The health and freedom it brought was a foretaste of the richness and depth of what salvation truly would accomplish for those who sought Him throughout the church age.

Even today, casting out the power of Satan from a life provides a basic, clean foundation from which to build the Christian way of living. This is pure salvation given by the Father to each person who chooses to take it as a gift from Him. In later years after Calvary where the blood of Christ purchased the authority over Satan, sin, death, and the world, He ascended to the right hand throne of the Father where He continues to intercede for us.

Exorcism is and has been traditionally practiced by Christ's ministers under His authority down through the centuries in and by His Church. It is used to either bring the unsaved to Christ or as cleansing to His children.

The deliverance ministry remains relevant and beneficial today in order for each child of God to:

1. Take a full position with God and His Christ.
2. Be healed in spirit, soul, and body.
3. Testify to the power of God which is alive and practical to this generation.
4. Move into the prosperity and blessings of God unhindered.
5. Serve as a means for gaining a lost world to Christ especially in missionary and outreach work.

Preliminary Steps To Deliverance

As a prayer counselor, you will encounter people who desire the ministry of deliverance. Having a desire or need for deliverance is not adequate for remaining delivered once they have been prayed for. And since God has an overall plan for each life and cannot be used to give instant relief for a problem, the beginning point for all deliverance is found in personal salvation. In fact, several preliminary actions must take place in and by the one requesting prayer.

In this regard, let me be clear on some basic meanings before we proceed. The words and meanings of deliverance and salvation in the original language are interchangeable in all aspects. They come from the Greek word *SOZO* "to save, deliver or protect, heal, preserve, to be made whole". *SOTERIA* is another word meaning "rescue or safety; health, salvation, saving, delivery, to save". *SOTARE* is a root word for "a deliverer", i.e., God in Jesus Christ.

To be saved means to be set completely free in your human spirit, soul, and body by an act of your will at God's invitation. It means turning away from sin and repenting to God for the inborn sin nature. It is done with an unconditional acceptance of Jesus Christ as a personal, life-giving Savior. This submission opens the unbeliever's spirit to life, to a renewing of the mind, and causes them to become born-again.

Christ's salvation includes deliverance from all evil spirits and their influences. By its very nature, salvation comes as a result of personal repentance from involvement in sin and a turning to Jesus Christ who provides continual cleansing throughout the lifetime. This is true salvation from the effects and consequences of the original sin nature. It is nurtured by the cleansing and washing Word of God and ministrations of the Holy Spirit enabling one to endure in all circumstances.

15

A Christian should not be living in a sinful condition after salvation but be righteous and upright before the Lord (1 John 3:7-10) without practiced sin. Any child of God can be free from habitual sin through the provision of repentance, confession and immediate cleansing and should, indeed, regard this as the "normal Christian life" Watchman Nee wrote about. It is true that all Christians continue to have a debased, sin-prone nature. That part will be redeemed when the body is resurrected; however, there is now, no domination of that nature as long as God's provision is appropriated as the need arises.

Deliverance is for those believers who have chosen the path of sin over God's perfect way and who need an "overhaul" by direct and immediate intervention of the Lord to get their life realigned. The deliverance ministry is not for the unsaved to become momentarily comfortable in their lost condition. Their most basic and pressing need is for salvation first which will take care of much of their difficulty and place them in a position for God's intervention to work for them.

"That if you confess WITH YOUR MOUTH, 'JESUS IS LORD', and BELIEVE IN YOUR HEART THAT GOD RAISED HIM FROM THE DEAD, YOU WILL BE SAVED. For it is with your heart that you believe and are justified, and it is with your mouth that you confess and are saved..for, EVERYONE WHO CALLS ON THE NAME OF THE LORD WILL BE SAVED." Rom 10:9-13, John 3:16-21, 1 John 5:1-5, 10-12.

As a counselor, make certain that *(1) he or she is a saved, believing Christian and that a public confession of this occurance has been made "with the mouth".* If you are dealing with someone who is unsaved, get this settled first or deliverance for them will be like pouring water through a hole-filled seive. It does little good at the time and will be detrimental in the long-run. However, some have been saved after seeing the power of Jesus Christ manifested to them. Generally, a public testimony of salvation happens at the time of water baptism for most believers.

Before deliverance takes place the prayer counselor should ask for a personal confession to be made out loud of their faith and desire to follow Christ and allow His Lordship over them. If they have not submitted to *(2) water baptism* in obedience to the Lord, ask the pastor to assist them with it as soon as possible.

Deliverance is a very serious grace and the counselee must be made aware of the scriptural order of a child of God. They should be in good faith with the Lord on the things He has told him or her to do (be saved/be baptized) before partaking of this ministry. Please take time at this preliminary stage to be assured in your own mind that those you pray with are fully strengthened and in obedience BEFORE deliverance. These basic steps are imperative to their spiritual position AFTER deliverance in order to maintain the holy ground newly won on the basis of their position of the beloved.

The third recommended preliminary action to deliverance is to *(3) seek and receive by faith the Baptism in the Holy Spirit.* There are scriptures cited concerning this experience. The Baptism in the Holy Spirit may be prayed for with the counseling team before or after deliverance. Be led of the Lord. It is a spiritual transaction that causes the counselee to be open to the Holy Spirit by a new flowing of his or her human spirit with God's.

It is important to understand that one does not receive the Holy Spirit when praying to receive the Baptism of the Holy Spirit. The Holy Spirit is given only once at the time of salvation. All the gifts of the Spirit are given when He comes into you at salvation for He is in full possession of them at all times and if He is indwelling, the gifts are already there. All believers are engifted at salvation: it is not a separate grace.

Let me clarify this by adding that receiving the Baptism of the Holy Spirit brings an acute awareness and receptive heart (mind) to Him to work as He sees fit in each believer. It is God's business to engift with whatever gift(s) He gives. The Baptism in the Holy Sprit is a refreshening to the human spirit to see and use the gifts already given. This may happen at the time of salvation, deliverance, during worship, water baptism, or anytime the Lord desires. It is taken by faith.

Being filled with the Holy Spirit of God is a highly joyous experience with some people speaking in other tongues. Others do not speak in tongues and it is not, by any means, a necessary occurance. BY FAITH, you receive baptism(s) in the Holy Spirit—not by emotion or instant gift manifestation. Look up John 20:19-22 and Acts 1:1-8, 2:1-4, 2:14-21, 8:14-17, 10:44-48, 19:1-7 for deeper understanding.

It is also good to realize and instruct the counselee that in the finished work of Jesus Christ at Calvary when His incorruptible blood was obediently given (John 19:30), that these specific works (and other, more numerous ones) were completed and paid for on behalf of all believers. Jesus gave us:

- Salvation from the consequences of natural sin and its curses.
- Salvation from death as a final Enemy-curse.

- Deliverance from the domination of sin, self, the world, Satan and all his devils.
- Healing (in spirit, soul, body) "..by His stripes we were healed" (Is 53:5), and by having a God-blessed life now.
- The imparting of the gifts of the Holy Spirit for ministry through the Baptism of the Holy Spirit (1 Cor 12, 13, 14).
- The opening of spiritual fellowship with the Trinity.

Salvation, deliverance, water baptism, and Spirit baptism must each be appropriated (taken as your own) to become active in your life. If your counselee has not experienced salvation or water baptism then you must help them seek and receive these two basic steps. This is a crucially important step in assisting them to find and obey Christ in two fundamental areas of discipleship.

At the close of a deliverance session, the counseling team should petition the Holy Spirit to minister as Healer and to fill and flow into all those places where the evil one was discharged. Be sure to terminate all sessions with a healing prayer, with joy, and the positive confession of God's unfailing love.

It should be a strong concern of the counselor that those prayed for become a committed member of a local church body where they can come under the discipline and blessing of the Word of God. It is here that added strength for continuing in the Christian walk under a shelter of spiritual protection and covering is available for on-going help and growth.

Some of you who are reading this manual will find a need for deliverance but may not have access to other Christians with whom to pray. Please do not undertake deliverance by yourself without the full protection of being saved and water baptized. Yet, even so, the Word of God given here will be quickened to the open heart for the Holy Spirit to minister directly to you. If you feel you need assistance for heavier deliverance or to share your experiences, there is an address given at the front of this manual where you may write to.

I cannot stress the necessity of being fully protected before submitting to deliverance. Jesus tells us in Matthew 12:43-45, that a person who gets incomplete, unprotected deliverance will be worse off by seven times with evil spirits re-entering. He or she must be in scriptural order before seeking deliverance. An "unoccupied house" is a person's spirit that is not inhabited by the Holy Spirit of God and is open to evil influence.

The following chart will help you focus these key events in your counselee's life and will be a good resource should Satan come to accuse them later with any disobedience. If the exact dates cannot be remembered, God knows them. If your counselee has any doubt on his or her part that these events occurred, encourage them to accept the Lord as Savior in front of you and suggest a fellowship where they may receive water baptism as a testimony of His grace

---

PLEASE FILL IN THESE BLANKS BEFORE GOING ON:

I know that I repented of my sin and accepted JESUS CHRIST as my

SAVIOR the approximate date of _____

I have been BAPTIZED IN WATER: Yes____ No____ When?_____

I have been BAPTIZED BY GOD'S HOLY SPIRIT: Yes____ No____

Signed:_____ Date:_____

CHAPTER 3

The Battleground
For Combat

Satan, as the god of this world system, is organized to continually set his will against God and God's children (James 4:4-7, 1 John 2:15-17). He is the archenemy of all that is good and of all that God favors. He uses or attempts to use the human spirit, soul, and body to exercise all or any control possible to enhance his own kingdom. The battle, however, IS WON OR LOST IN YOUR MIND AND BY YOUR WILL, not by some wiley devil with a bag of tricks. All combat with Satanic forces begins and continues in the arena of the mind.

The human tripartite in which the battle is raged, shows the effects of the struggle for control or the lack of it. In each person, without exception, there is predominantly either a wealth of peace, love, joy, and health clearly discernable, or else cursed living exhibited by depression, disease, failure, and "bad luck" that haunts almost every move. These are the cutting edges of the battle. It is here where the scars of successful soldiers of the cross are created, or where the losses of defeat are revealed.

To assess the spiritual damage in one's self and join in to literally fight for a life of peace and joy, we must first recognize exactly where Satan is waging war. Is it from within or without? Are Godward efforts resisted by his constant accusations to the Father against you? Or are the vile vexations of his demon horde consistently at your mind to tempt and throw you off God's plan for your life?

It is only when we learn to recognize in our spirits what is of Jehovah God, what is of the human spirit, and what is of self and of Satan, that we can begin to agree with the Lord in being and remaining overcomers. We must recognize what a battle is before any prayer counseling can be done to bring others to that light.

The spiritual victory has already been freely gifted to each Christian but at an exorbitantly high price to the person of Jesus Christ. It cost Him His very life to ensure that His children could be delivered from all the on-slaught of the enemy. And to claim that deliverance requires one to get the reality of what the cross-victory encompasses. This knowledge will produce the basis for becoming an overcomer of the world, over your flesh, and certainly over Satan. We will begin that process in this chapter.

The Four Mind Attitudes Of God's Order

1. THE MIND MUST BE CHANGED. The unregenerate (natural, unsaved) mind which is the self-nature, is hostile toward God and utterly unable to subject itself to God's laws (Romans 8:5-7). The natural mind rejects the true teachings of God because it perceives them as foolishness (1 Cor 2:14). Unless this kind of mind is changed, a person cannot get his or her thoughts off the pleasures and problems of life and will remain occupied with the cares of the world and not with pleasing God. The unchanged mind never comes to salvation.

REPENTANCE—to radically change one's mind—is a gift from God and an act of faith. It is the decision at God's prompting to stop the self-nature (fleshly) behavior, and turn to God with the whole mind and heart. Repentance recognizes the human inability to help oneself in any way with salvation. It is the decision not only to turn away from sin, but to turn to the Lord and His purposes for that life. After repentance, the Changed Mind begins a spiritual relationship with Christ because the human spirit has been birthed.

CHRISTIANITY IS NOT A RELIGION: IT IS A RELATION-SHIP WITH GOD IN THE PERSON OF JESUS CHRIST UNDER THE CARE OF THE HOLY SPIRIT.

---

2. THE MIND MUST BE RENEWED. *"..be ye transformed by the renewing of your mind* (Romans 12:2). The Renewed Mind has the attitude of God's will. We are commanded to "..PUT OFF your old self, which is being corrupted by its deceitful desires; ..be made new in the attitude of your minds; and PUT ON the new self, created to be like God in true righteousness and holiness" (Eph 4:22-24). The translator uses the Greek word *ANANEOO* in this passage by which we see the intention to "renovate, reform, make new again".

The renewing process is an on-going endeavor in the Christian walk. It is this Renewed Mind that causes us to look and behave in "Christ-likedness". It is the image of Jesus Christ found in His true children which displays the fruit of the Holy Spirit (Galations 5:22-25).

3. THE MIND MUST BE CONTROLLED. First Peter 1:13 says, *"..prepare your minds for action; be self-controlled; set your hope fully on the grace to be given you..."* In 2 Corinthians 10 verse 5 (KJV), we are told, "Casting down imaginations..and bringing into captivity every thought to the obedience of Christ". The Self-controlled Mind keeps us balanced and poised for godliness and reinforces the Renewed Mind by not allowing either passivity or fanaticism access to the spirit.

4. THE MIND MUST BE OCCUPIED BY GODLY THOUGHTS. A blank, uninvolved mind produces a passive will that Satan takes rapid advantage of. Philippians 4:8 tells us to *"..think on what is pure."* THINK, in this verse, is a command of active engagement. Again, in Colossians 3:1-2, we are told to *"SET your mind on things which are above, where Christ is seated at the right hand of God..not on earthly things".*

The God-centered mind, therefore, is an active, doing mind, able to defeat outside attempts by evil tormentors and continue to build and nourish the Renewed Mind by its athletic vigilance. A Godly Mind loves to memorize and live by Scripture. It craves God's fellowship and nourishment.

EVERY THOUGHT SUGGESTED TO THE MIND BY EVIL SPIRITS AND ACCEPTED, IS GROUND GIVEN TO THEM. ANY UNUSED OR MISUSED MIND INVITES THE ATTEMPTED USE OF IT BY DEMONIC POWERS.

The preceeding four controls of anyone's mind will be stronger or weaker depending on what that person chooses to be of most importance to them. Do they wish to remain unsaved? They choose to have an Unchanged Mind. Have they decided with God's grace to repent when confronted with sin? Then they have chosen to possess a Renewed Mind. What about the Christian who fills his or her mind with soap-operas, junk reading, and mindless chatter? These have set themselves to be undisciplined and uncontrolled in their thinking. It just seems easier for them to ride through life with a minimal commitment to Christ and foolishly "let things happen".

And next we have believers who are seriously pursuing the Lord in a personal, one-on-one relationship. Not only do they not allow superficial fluff or outright garbage into their thought processes, but have taken every opportunity to fill their minds with the Word, annointed music, edifying company, and spirit-building books, sermons, and tapes.

Let's turn our attention to the following seven mind-sets (thinking processes) which are battlegrounds for Satan and his minions. Remember, to the degree a person has yielded ground or has not come out of a negative mind posture, will determine the extent of control he or she has allowed Satan to maintain within.

Minds That Are Battlegrounds

The Corrupted Mind. At this stage, unbelievers are at the complete mercy of Satan. This mind is fleshly, unregenerate, and is naturally set to war against the Spirit of God. It gives the enemy total access to this person. The Corrupted Mind is a dead mind to the Holy Spirit and is thoroughly saturated in the world system and bent on destruction. It cannot know God.

The Ignorant Mind. A person with an Ignorant Mind does not and cannot believe God's truth because they are unaware of what Truth is. They lack knowledge and experience with Truth. This is not sinful in itself, but it is a state of mind. It is foolish to retain an Ignorant Mind because Truth will be confused with a lie, good looks evil, and wrongs seem to be rights. By not exploring God's Word, the Ignorant Mind chooses to go its own way. It is the most dangerous mind set because it often reacts to circumstance instead of acting from conviction, decisiveness, and knowledge.

The Blinded Mind. Second Corinthians 3:14 and 4:4 tells us that those of the world have been blinded by the god of light against the gospel of Jesus Christ. Satan is in the business to blind minds where all change occurs. The Blinded Mind is found in unbelievers who can sit under the Gospel yet never hear or understand it. The Blinded Mind is a state that can be broken in the unsaved by a witness who will press through to their salvation.

In the believer, a Blinded Mind is seen in a person's refusal to deal with particular sins of commission or omission that are painfully obvious to others in the Body, or by rejecting what is truly the will of God for them when it conflicts with their perceptions of Truth. Spiritual blindness is repented of.

Chapter 3

The Unrenewed Mind. This mind-set belongs to a "baby" or spiritually undeveloped Christian who has not or has only partially given his or her mind to the Lord to renew (Romans 12:1-2). Persisting with an unrenewed, worldly mind is dangerous fence-sitting ground, making it difficult to tell these people (the wheat) from the world (tares). An Unrenewed Mind is Satan's playpen and if continued in by rebellion or by passively refusing God's ways, can result in the loss of that person's faith to believe God in His fullness. This is usually a transitory stage or perhaps a momentary period in one who accepts Christ and immediately passes into eternity by death.

The Depraved Mind. Romans 1:28-32 explains the Depraved Mind which is a result of *"..since they did not THINK it worthwhile to retain the knowledge of God, He gave them over to a depraved mind..."* Those with Depraved Minds do what ought not to be done; are full of envy, murder, strife, deceit, malice and are gossips, slanderers, God-haters, insolent, arrogant and boastful. They invent ways of doing evil; disobey their parents, and are senseless, faithless, heartless, and ruthless. The Depraved Mind is marked by moral corruption, is evil, and totally sets self against God. It thrives on willful rebellion.

The Suggestible Mind. Suggestions are not truths. Suggestions are the hint, the intimation, the insinuation, the implication to truth. A suggestion is a seduction. Christians who do not search out Truth are, or increasingly become gullible, easily believing whatever they are told especially if it sounds "religious". Satan, as the father of all lies, delights to prophesy to humans who are naturally curious and receptive—especially to suggestions about future events or personal circumstance. Fostering a Suggestible Mind leads to deeply harmful paths of deception and is difficult to be renewed because of its natural bent to comfortable, easily held and not-thought-through beliefs.

The Passive Mind. Christians, use your minds! The mind must be actively engaged. One signal that a mind is passive shows itself as inactive when action is called for. Or by behaving in rash or over-reactive ways after long periods of operating from indecisiveness. This allows unnecessary frustration to build then explode in the flesh. The passive mind is unwatchful, displays a lack of concentration, uses poor or no judgment, had a bad memory, and is easily confused. See Matthew 13:23 and Isaiah 26:3.

Areas that can be turned over by passivity are: the will, emotions, judgment and reasoning abilities; the conscience, spirit, body, whole personality, imagination, and creativity. The Passive Mind does not attain to full personhood because few stands which would build character, are taken. Evil spirits are able to both impart ideas to men and women with passive minds and steal ideas away from them (Luke 8:12). The Passive Mind does not live in reality, will not confront a bad situation headon, and is oblivious of things in life that others are acutely aware of.

THE PRIMARY CAUSE OF DECEPTION AND POSSESSION OF DEMONIC INFLUENCE IS FROM THE MIND(S) THAT GIVES GROUND FOR THEIR OPERATIONS. THE AMOUNT OF RIGHTS YIELDED TO THEM DETERMINES THE AMOUNT AND TYPE OF ACTIVITY THEY ARE FREE TO TORMENT WITH.

The most basic and consequential law of the spirit realm is that nothing pertaining to a person, either for or against them, can be accomplished WITHOUT THE CONSENT OF HIS OR HER WILL. To recover lost territory previously given over to the enemy means that an exercise of the person's will by repentance with an insistance on the lordship of Jesus Christ. The Lord in this way assumes rule over the territory with no further tolerance of demonic activity permitted (Romans 7:25 and 12:2).

This is an example of the use of a directed, Active Mind that is aggressively willing and able to make those definite decisions to follow Christ that are primary to knowing and obeying God in a purposeful manner. This Active Mind is pleasing to the Father, and indeed, thirsts after Him to know Him ever better.

The next chapter shows us a picture of the enemy and what the open doors are that would allow his devious attacks. Seek the Lord to take from you any blindness in preconceived ideas about Satan and allow the Holy Spirit to place the lamp before your feet as you go step by step into the knowledge of the enemy.

CHAPTER 4

The Nature and
Activity of Demons

What is natural to a demon? How do they act and react? What are their tasks to perform for their master, and how does this impact on Christians who are in the world which lies in the hands of the wicked one? Let's take a look from Scripture at their attributes and abilities. Demons have:

1. Knowledge. Matthew 8:28-32; Mark 1:24.
2. A Will. Matthew 12:43-45; Luke 11:14-15.
3. Emotions. James 2:18-19; Luke 9:39-43.
4. The ability to speak, cry, wail, shriek, shake people violently, recognize Jesus Christ as the Holy One of God, obey the commands of Jesus and depart. Mark 1:23-28.
5. Self-awareness. Mark 5:6-10.
6. Power to inhabit idols as gods. Deuteronomy 32:16-21.
7. Authority to inhabit humankind. Luke 22:3-6.
8. Drive people into solitary places. Luke 11:24-26.
9. Teach deceit through hypocritical liars. 1 Tim 4:1-5.
10. Perform miraculous signs. Revelation 16:13-14.

These are characteristics of a living, viable personality. Demons are spirits. They are not now, nor have ever been, human. They are not ghosts of people who have died. Indeed, they have no concept of or experience with being eligible for salvation through Christ as all humankind has. They do, however, seek people, animals, and objects through which to show their presence and power.

A demonic spirit's primary objective is to destroy the peace and harmony of any union a person has with the Holy Trinity. Then they begin to introduce as much temptation to sin, anguish, guilt, grief, misfortune, curse, privation, disease, anxiety, fear and confusion as allowed into that life to keep the believer's spiritual unity with the Lord interrupted.

Satan commissions his emissaries of evil to be themselves. That means their nature is to seduce, entice to sin, confuse, lie, manifest themselves and drive, perverting all that is natural in assisting their king to lead the whole world astray: one person and one nation at a time.

When not inhabiting within, Satan and his demonic scabs wander through deserted places. Why do you think Jesus Christ was sent by the Holy Spirit into the desert forty days? Satan was there to tempt him; He was out there with wild animals and angels, attending him (Mark 1:12-13). We have no idea what lengths Jesus Christ was pushed to, but He overcame every temptation to evil! And, the battle is there for each of us until we go home when Father calls us. Until then, the victorious Christian learns to fight back in the power and might of the Holy Spirit and in the name of Jesus. He is our example.

Attacks Against The Innerman

The most common symptoms indicating the presence and activities of demons are found in humankind's two most basic areas of the innerman of soul (the will, mind, and emotions) and against the physical body. For further study in this area, may I suggest the book, *"War On The Saints,"* by Jesse Penn-Lewis. She faced spiritual warfare after the Welsh revival about 100 years ago and what she writes about it is as valid today as it was then.

Demonic manifestations in the oppressed person against the innerman may come in several forms. Some will be obvious and aggressive while others will scarcely be seen. Some can only be revealed by the use of the gifts of the Spirit. Included here is a compilation that serves as a partial revelation to their varied attack forms.

1. Persistent or recurrent evil or destructive emotions and attitudes that can dominate a person even contrary to his or her own will: resentment, fears, hatred, envy, jealousy, pride, self-pity, tension, suicide, anger, impatience, rejection, meanness, a bullying attitude or actions, filth and abusiveness, rage and a lack of conscience.

2. Moods which are unreasonable or sudden with extreme fluctuations: open to depression or high euphoria. Alcohol, all drugs, rock music, and pornography open the door to moods. People can become double-minded (lose their identity), confused, irrational, and diseased.

3. Various forms of religious error: bondage and submission to unscrip-

tural doctrines and/or groups, cults, ideologies; included are all types of material and psychological idolatry, false worship, and attraction to error.

4. Resorting to charms and luck: fortune telling, astrology, mediums and cultic idols and symbols (Appendix IV, Glossary).

5. Enslaving personal habits: nicotine and tars, gluttony, compulsion to be overly thin or fat, the abuse of alcohol, illegal or prescriptive drugs, sugar-craving, caffeine-laden drinks or medicines; a mania for television and worldly entertainment, ungodly music, gambling, and like habits.

6. Unclean language: blasphemy, mockery, dirty joking, gossip, idle empty talk; a compulsion to constant talk or activity.

7. Uncontrollable perversions of all kinds: sexual immorality, rape, evil sex-oriented materials, videos, photos, and literature; child porn and all sexual activity with children or animals.

8. Persistent or violent opposition to the truth of Scripture, to the Name of Jesus Christ, to the only wise God, or against the Church (body of believers worldwide).

9. Adherance to worldly wisdom: psychological self-help books and articles that set the mind against God's ways or will; hypnotism, subliminal suggestions, extreme body fixations, mind control, "success-motivation" theories, Dr. Ruth-type books or videos, psychiatry as the answer, mind channelers, spirit guides.

10. Activist or Rights groups that are opposed to the Word of God and its teachings: rebellion against Godly spiritual, parental, or governing authorities.

11. Prostitution of the innerman: trading or giving part of one's self away for unseemly gain by commercializing a God-given ministry, the intellect, or spiritual gifts.

Attacks Against The Physical Body

The following partial list are symptoms that have been seen or can be expected to be seen in people who are demonized. Many are especially evident when the evil spirits have been stirred up by the Name and power of God. They will react in these ways through the person being delivered.

It is possible that some of these actions will be threatened against the counselee or prayer counselor, but be assured that nothing Satanic can stand against or harm the child of God who is utterly trusting in Him for safety.

1. Unnatural restlessness, talkativeness, muttering, yawning, flailing of arms, head, or legs; crawling into a fetal position.

2. Glazed eyes (dull) or overly bright and protruding; the inability to focus naturally, to keep their eyes open when spoken to (demons are trying to hide), eyes that snap with anger or hatred, weeping and pleading.

3. Froth at the mouth, fetid breath, over-salivating, vomiting, burping, gasiness, blasphemous language, threats of death or harm, begging to remain; the inability to speak the names of Jesus Christ, God the Father, the Holy Spirit, Trinity; accusations against those participating in the deliverance.

4. Palpitations: unnaturally accelerated or slowed heart beat, flushed skin, welts, bruises, bites and scratch marks.

5. Shunning, recoiling from or fighting against the power of the Holy Spirit; cowering in a corner or under coverings.

6. Unnatural coldness in the extremities or in the room because of the presence of evil; hair or skin bumps rising involuntarily, and a sense in the human spirit of unrest and disorder.

7. Demons have admitted to causing mental and physical infirmities (Luke 13:11) such as: insanity, infection, heart disease, cancers, tumors, ulcers, arthritis, paralysis, deafness, blindness, insomnia, epilepsy, catatonia, and rape of both males and females.

How May Satan Enter To Torment?

THROUGH FLESHLY OR SOULISH ACTIVITY. God does not destroy the human will at salvation. We are forever left with the ability to choose to serve self through carnal pleasures or to serve God in righteousness. Satan will dominate the area(s) of any life willed to him such as through lusts, pride, love of money, or any attraction to the world system he controls.

Christians must not entertain thoughts concerning anything contrary to the will of God as revealed in His Word, for evil spirits will dominate those areas as time and space is given for their development. Ignorance is not an excuse. Time must be set aside for the study of God's Word.

Some entertain sin so long, roots and inroads into the personality are formed. Deception can thus come that that sin is "just a part of me". Besetting sin becomes an excuse like, "she's always crabby in the morning—that's just how she is". Or, "John is a fighter. He's a red head, isn't he?" Another deception that is thought to be part and parcel of the personality is homosexuality which is not natural as no one is "born with it", and is not just another thing to "understand" about someone. Homosexuality is an evil root that can be cast out of a life.

Demons who do reside, reveal themselves through activity in the body. It happens through a series of events which begins in the mind by thinking on a particular wickedness. That becomes a recurring temptation over time as it is mentally caressed and toyed with before a decision to do it is reached. Then, one day, it is acted out by decision and becomes full-blown sin. Persisting in sin invites demonic control because that is their realm. They will help you persist in sin until it becomes the idol that replaces the living God. And that monster will disable you for God's service and kingdom living. That is living in sin.

Idol worship is spiritual sin accomplished through taking a soulish avenue. It is the turning FROM God for righteousness, direction, answers, and provision of needs TO relying on spirit or human forces for those same needs. This sin will bring forth fruit unto death (Romans 5:12-14).

THROUGH REBELLIOUS ACTIVITIES. "For rebellion is as the sin of witchcraft, and stubbornness is as iniquity and idolatry." (1 Samuel 15:23 KJV). Rebellion and stubbornness, evident in both soul and body, are equated with witchcraft and idolatry which are sins of the human spirit and are eventually manifested by the soul and body.

Rebellion is seen in the invention of new ways to do evil: in terrorism, bombing of civilians and children, shooting innnocent people on highways for traffic infractions, hijacking, hostage taking, political violence, racism, physical and psychological torture, abortion as birth control or sex selection, prison and work camp extermination, cannibalism of human body parts, the buying and selling of children or adults, planned famine for political or material gain, conceiving children just to sell for profit or give to Satan in worship.

Murder and suicide are rebellion before God because someone who wishes to commit either act states in effect, "I WILL take my own life or another's life when I WANT TO, not when God ordains it to end. This attempts to set one on the level of God ("I have power over life like God"). It is pure blasphemy. Suicide leads to final separation from God because it is the only sin that cannot be repented of in this life (dead people cannot repent). See 1 Corinthians 3:16-17 for your own interpretation of this.

THROUGH ABNORMAL SEXUAL ACTIVITY. Sex with animals; sex with or between children, incest, consenting to sex with demons as in Satanic rites. Homosexual and lesbian behavior is not natural and is against God's order of "...be fruitful and multiply". See 2 Kings 23:7, Romans 1:21-27, Leviticus 18:22-23, Jude 6-8, Exodus 22:19, and Deut 23:17.

THROUGH THE FAMILY LINES. All types of sicknesses, nervous conditions, alcoholism, mental illness, rejection, hatred against loved ones, emotional soul-ties, fears, and other abnormal or negative attitudes may be passed along through the family chain which could be centuries long. God promised that curses would continue to the third and fourth generations. For this reason it is possible to see unusual demonic activity in the lives of those of the fourth generation in order to continue the curse chain.

THROUGH A CRITICAL SPIRIT. Slandering, lying under oath, vain babbling (confusion of sounds or voices), gossip, foolish jesting that is profane or sarcastic. Unfair or untrue criticism against fellow Christians and others will cut you off from God's blessing. This is verbal hatred and cursing—while set against another (who is probably trying as seriously as you are to follow God)—will block YOU from the Lord. First John 3:15 says, "Anyone who hates his brother is a murderer, and you know that no murderer has eternal life in him."

THROUGH WORRYING. Giving into worry as a way of life demands that you stay in charge of the situation and control it yourself (by worrying it through) instead of putting your faith in God and patiently allowing Him to act. Negative people draw many problems to themselves and keep those problems alive by seeking the spirit of worry for comfort "in trials". Worry brings on destruction to internal organs, sickness, and premature death.

THROUGH LAZINESS OR OVERWORK. The spirits of laziness and tiredness sometimes enter together and connote a lack of self-control and discipline. Some lazy Christians are deceived into believing that their inactivity is actually "waiting on the Lord" or "letting the Lord move". God moves through the active mind, not the lazy mind.

It is natural and normal to make mistakes in all of life because we continue to be learners, so keep on trying after the most glaring mistakes! Keep in mind that if a ship does not even have its keel in the water going in some direction (even the wrong one), God cannot move on its behalf to get it going in His direction. Laziness or fear to move is never honored by God.

Overwork can also invite tormenting spirits because one's physical resistance is lowered making it easier to give in to negative suggestions. Workaholic and over-achiever behavior is sin and rebellion against God's natural laws of needing rest, a change of pace, and reflective time for God and family.

Both extremes result in bodily or emotional overload. God's way is orderly and balanced. He will never drive you because He expects to be asked to do for you. Work is a true blessing: self-abuse by overwork or lack of work does not please Him and will not produce His best in you.

THROUGH CULTS AND THE OCCULT. Occultism is the belief that supernatural powers can be brought under human control. Those who participate (even "innocently") become like the thing they do (1 Cor 10:21-22, Deut 5:7,9). The occult is strickly forbidden to Christians.

What does God mean when He speaks of the occult as an abomination? In Old Testament Hebrew, the words *TOEBAH, PIGGUL,* and *SHEQETS* were used to mean "filthy, loathing, pollution, idolatrous; to stink, be unclean, unceremonial, disgusting, abhorrent of; and to an idol, idolatry. A hidden thing is an abominable custom or object to the Lord". This is rather strong language to use to demonstrate God's displeasure.

The occult (hidden) is an abomination because it is the attempt to attract seducing spirits and Satanic powers. It is the seeking of guidance from sources other than from the Lord. Our Father, however, is a jealous God who wants to provide for and love His own children ONLY through His own resources and methods.

OCCULTISM IS IDOLATRY. IT DOES NOT MATTER THAT
YOU THINK YOU ARE JUST PLAYING AROUND OR IT
REALLY DOESN'T MEAN ANYTHING TO YOU. THERE IS
NO INNOCENT PARTICIPATION IN THE OCCULT. IT IS SIN.

Cult (system of formal unorthodox religious beliefs based on a human
or religious figure) and occult involvement hardens the unbeliever and
curious Christian against the Gospel causing him or her to resist the Word
of God. This happens because the human spirit is being fixed in unbelief
and rebellion through false dogma. How a home, child's room, vehicle,
and your person are decorated and clothed often indicates spiritual doors
that have been opened to the Satanic (Deut 7:25-26). See Appendix III.

THROUGH REJECTION AND SELF-PITY. The positive element
of rejection that the Christian adopts comes against the world, Satan, and
sin, acting as an anchor to the straight and narrow path of God. In its negative connotation, rejection is pitted against the soul (self); especially when
the emotions say "I am inferior, unworthy, my body is not right, no one
loves me, I don't deserve to know God," and other such lies. Rejection is
one of the strongest forms of hatred possible.

Rejection directed against others is manifested in physical isolation
either as punishment or as a withdrawal of the self to control others. It is
seen in ignoring "them" through direct attack by destablilizing relationships, as over-protection, in love of things or pets rather than in love of people, and in the inability to be vulnerable and open to change.

The spirit of self-pity often enters with rejection when a person accepts
Satan's lies as truth and "feels sorry" for the self. These family spirits
strengthen and reinforce each other within the victim, creating a circle of
energy. The main key to handling rejection is found in forgiving which will
be explained in detail in Chapter 7. See Romans 15:7, Psalm 27:10 and
100:3, Isaiah 44:24, Exodus 4:11, Ephesians 1:6b, and Revelation 4:11.

THROUGH PROSTITUTION. This area includes physical, sexual
prostitution with males and/or females. It covers emotional, mental, and
human spirit prostitution wherein one gives over or sells that which belongs to God (your life, walk, family, physical and emotional health,
finances, possessions, service or ministry, and spiritual gifts) in order to
personally gain something of value to you.

The word prostitute in Hebrew is *CHALAL* meaning "to wound, dissolve, to profane a person, place, or thing; to break one's word, to begin as if by an opening wedge, to play, defile, break, eat a common, unclean thing; to take an inheritance, pollute or profane self in prostitution; to slay, cause sorrow, stain, and grieviously harm". See Ezekiel 23.

THROUGH NEGATIVE DEMONIC CONFESSIONS OF THE MOUTH. Proverbs 18:21 says, *"The tongue has the power of life and death".* Curses against God and others either spoken, written, or thought, are vessels of supernatural power which tend to continue through time until they are revoked and broken. People, Satan, or you can initiate these negative demonic confessions that will work against you and your family.

Curses that are over you will produce humiliation, failure to reproduce physically, mentally, or spiritually; will bring on sicknesses, family breakdown, poverty, defeat, oppression, failure, Godly and secular disfavor. It will cause a person to be the "tail (one who is led about) and not the head (one who is the leader)" in life's endeavors (Deut 28:13,44). Using or being used by negative demonic confession will bring one into Satan's stronghold and certain ruin.

THROUGH ABNORMAL, PROLONGED GRIEF. Grief is a natural outlet given by God in times of loss, stress, repentance, and for healing. When grief is abused and used as a crutch instead of allowing the Lord to be the source of all comfort, an opening to self-pity, bitterness, sarcasm (the power or will to cut and sting), cynicism, and ultimately the questioning of God's purposes, will appear.

Mourning is given for a season. It is not a way of life for the Christian. It definitely is not to be used as a ploy for getting or keeping affection (James 1:2-5).

THROUGH FEAR. Unnatural fears are torments sent by Satan (1 John 4:18). The love of God casts out all fear. Giving in to fear closes off God's peace and joy and blocks your faith from moving the mountain that stands between you and blessings.

Fear produces insecurity, causes moral decay, uses rationalism instead of realism, draws loved ones into the same perilous net, and freezes one into inactivity where Satan works best, instead of to action where God works. The Word says, "..what is feared is what is worshipped". We are told to fear (highly reverence) only Jehovah God in Isaiah 8:13, Proverbs 29:25, and Psalm 34:4.

THROUGH DENOMINATIONAL AND RELIGIOUS DECEPTION AND DOGMA. We are to be completely free in Jesus Christ so as not to abide under religious law. Bad theology and false teaching come from the angel of light (2 Cor 11:14), and twists the good Word of God. We tend to resist change under the impression that what we now have is the whole truth; which of course, cannot be valid because Truth is living and Christians are ever learning.

The Christian with set and cemented beliefs will dangerously limit himself to hearing and receiving what he currently believes. A rigid belief system that comes through denominational lines limits the Holy Spirit within the believer to receive new Truth. This is illustrated quite well in the movement of the Holy Spirit (with the evidence of speaking in tongues in some) during the late 1960's and early 1970's in the United States. Many were so dedicated to their denominational stand on this issue that they taught against it to the division of the Church. But did they take time to listen to the Lord about it? He can be counted on to constantly lift Jesus higher as He moves in His overall plan for these last days. We must be careful not to speak against anything we have not heard directly from Him about.

Holy Scripture, and not any cult's various bibles, is the final authority for doctrine. The Holy Spirit agrees with the Word of God so He CANNOT blaspheme Himself. That means that everything you now believe to be true should be held up to the scrutiny of the Word of God for "..teaching, rebuking, correcting, and training in righteousness, so that the man of God may be thoroughly equipped for every good work" (2 Tim 2:16-17).

If you are a member of a religious order or organization that cannot be questioned, whose leadership is under no higher authority, or which has no Scriptural basis, you are in error.

THROUGH THE MIND-SET THAT IS UNDISCIPLINED FOR GOD. See Chapter 3 for clarification of the seven mind battlegrounds and their ramifications.

THROUGH FANTASY, DELUSIONS, EUPHORIA PRODUCED BY DRUGS, OR VAIN IMAGINATIONS. Do not confuse these soulish entrances through which Satan enters with God-given creativity or valid visions (these are generally rare and must be Scripture-tested), or by mountain-moving faith. God's mode of entrance does not come through the soul or body (as Satan's does), but through the human spirit communing with His Holy Spirit.

THROUGH UNGODLY TYPES OF MUSIC. Mark 4:25 (NAS) says to *". .take care what you listen to".* Worldly music keeps the heart and mind centered on humanity: on his abilities, lusts, and preoccupations with love and success. New Age music and pagan (much oriental, native beat) music is not from our Father.

Hard and acid rock and the newer varieties contain teaching, seduction, appealing emphasis on illicit sex, drugs, demons, witchcraft, murder, suicide, violence, uncleanness, visual repugnance and filthiness. Any music that is vulgar, destructive, blanks the mind, damages the sense of hearing from its loudness, causes people to become spasmodic or entranced, or lose self-control is of the devil.

Be especially careful of "christian" music that is worldly in lyrics, beat, and dress that lures believers into worldliness, rebellion, and self-centeredness. Phil Driscoll does an excellent service to the Lord in stating that any music (no matter what it sounds like) that lifts up, magnifies, and centers worship on the Lord Jesus Christ is of Him. Throw away even "gospel" music if it is Scriptually off and doesn't magnify our Lord. Be astute and alert. Guard your spirit to listen to annointed music whereby it serves as a barrier in the heavenlies so our praises can be raised for battle.

THROUGH CURIOSITY IN SPIRITISM AND DEMONOLOGY. *"Take heed that you be not ensnared to follow them (pagans) after they have been destroyed before you, and that you do not inquire about their gods, saying, 'How did these nations serve their gods?' "* (Deut 12:30).

Idle curiosity in Satanism, the occult, through reading of New Age or other cult materials, in what psychics, channelers, and spirit guides say, and in any demonic activity, gives place to spiritual and mental strongholds not easily broken. We should, however, be very well versed in the Word on what God says about Satan, the occult, and the demonic. We are to know the enemy but not get it from his press agents.

THROUGH RELIGIOUS PICTURES, STATUES, AND IMAGES. *"The images of their gods you are to burn in the fire. Do not covet the silver and gold on them, and do not take it for yourselves, or you will be ensnared by it for it is detestable to the Lord your God. Do not bring a detestable thing into your house or you, like it, will be set apart for destruction. Utterly abhor and detest it, for it is set apart for destruction".* See Deut 7:25-26.

Pastor Cho of Korea gives warning that all Buddhas, oriental, African, and primitive art decorations represent many demons that we of the western nations may not be aware of. These are not to be purchased at all, and if purchased, destroyed outright. According to Deuteronomy, we are not to give them away or sell them to others, either. In fact, demonic pictures, statues, obscene works of art and images give power to the enemy to indwell them. Many times when any kind of Godly ministry is attempted in a room, home, or office having these objects, the working of God is hindered because of the shared strength between these familiar objects.

"You shall not make for yourself an idol in the form of ANYTHING IN HEAVEN ABOVE or ON THE EARTH beneath or IN THE WATERS BELOW. You shall not bow down to them or worship them; for I, the Lord your God, am a jealous God, punishing the children for the sin of the fathers to the third and fourth generation of those who hate me, but showing love to a thousand generations of those who LOVE ME AND KEEP MY COMMANDMENTS." Exodus 20:4-6.

You can see that the above verses include all so-called "christian" or religious images, statues, jewelry, and symbols. God is a Spirit and He wants to be worshipped in spirit and in truth. He cannot be relegated to human or earthly forms and symbols. See Acts 19:19, Deut 12:2-3, 2 Kings 18:4, and Jude 8:27.

This sketch on the demonic nature and powers is not meant to be exhaustive. There are many fine books written about where evil spirits come from and their hierarchical structuring (Billy Graham did one on "Angels"). But it is meant to give an idea of their personalities, objects of conquest, and powers related to the deliverance ministry.

Do you now have on your helmet of salvation? Are you girded with the belt of Truth and dressed in the breastplate of righteousness? If so, get ready to raise your shield of faith against the fiery darts of Satan who is already crashing against the spirits, souls, and bodies of all Christians. This is the subject of our next three chapters.

Chapter 5

The Attack Against
The Human Spirit

God created humans as tripartite beings (composed of three parts) and in His likeness as He is three in one, the Trinity. We are made of:

(1) *SPIRIT* or "heart", able to respond to God and to the spiritual (God's Spirit, demonic spirits, and other human spirits);

(2) the *SOUL* or "mind, will, intellect and emotions" able to respond in human relationships out of a personality that can think, make decisions, and has feelings; and

(3) *BODY,* the physical external body with senses of touch, taste, smell, hearing, and sight that are tuned into maintaining physical life and surviving in an earth-bound environment.

The point of salvation is when personal repentance for past sin is made along with the confession that Jesus Christ is God's only Son. The Father gives His faith for this human response to salvation. It is this new birth of restoring the human spirit to contact with God that had been forfeited by the first Adam in Eden.

When the human spirit is birthed anew (Jn 3:1-21) and united with the Lord of Glory and begins to grow in spiritual power, the less able it is to come under the control of the spirits of darkness. Therefore, we in being renewed spiritual creatures, are translated out of the kingdom of darkness into the kingdom of God's Son. It is a spiritual transaction. Likewise the soul and body which had before been totally open to the poison of Satan, learns how to shut down to Satanic influence as the new spirit rules under the Holy Spirit's direction. This is how in Christ Jesus one becomes united as a whole spirit, soul, and body forged into a vital unit ready for God's higher purposes and indeed, spiritual warfare.

During the time a person is spiritually dead to Jehovah God before this rebirth milestone, the human spirit is nevertheless, able to communicate with demonic forces, have spiritual experiences, and be controlled by netherworld forces sometimes manifested in signs and wonders, psychic abilities, and mind control of others. Those who follow non-Christian religions, gurus, and overt Satanic societies do have "spiritual" contact — but not with our Lord.

For those spiritually dead to God, the door that must be opened in reaching the Almighty Eternal One is only provided in Christ Jesus. He is the Door, the latch, the keyhole, the hinges, the bolts, the Everything! This is what intercessory prayer for deliverance is all about. Translating from darkness into Light.

The counselor begins by first offering salvation to those hopelessly seeking wrong gods in improper ways. Even if it is someone you know and had thought were saved. Press in here by helping him or her find Jesus, the Only Christ. It is at this point that a division between living in the renewed spirit and dealing with the soul-life is made. While by the sword of the Holy Spirit this distinction is made, each person must consent with his will to the process.

Let me pose a question and answer it that will help clarify the necessity for division of spirit from soul in the counselee. What is it about the expression of the soul that separates a person from walking in the Spirit?. Chiefly, there are these things:

1. It is in the soul area (mind, afffections, emotions, will, intellect) that sin is wrestled with. When a person knows that he or she must take up the cross of Christ—denying the pleasure of the soul to have its own way—a clash comes between the human spirit and the Holy Spirit who requires the Cross life (Mt 10:38). For instance, Christ says we are to leave our father and mother and follow Him. A choice must be made. The family or Christ.

Now is when the soul puts up a mighty fight to keep the family. The sword of the Lord comes through to divide this soul-position from the God-position. But it can only happen with the person's consent. The beauty of this is in seeing the affections of the soul put under subjection to the Lordship of Christ: the lower life exchanged for the higher. Thus, the soul is dominated by the spirit which wishes to comply with the Holy Spirit. And with the soul in its proper order, God can move and bless so that he no longer loves his family with human, frail love, but has exchanged it for the love of God toward them.

2. Matthew 16:24-26 says that if any would come after me, let him deny himself...For whosoever would save his life (psuche-soul) shall lose it: and whosoever would lose his life (psuche-soul) shall find it. Now, here is

the soul-life summed up in the one word "himself". It is the fleshly self-life that is contrary to not only God's will, but is against its own best interests. The sword of the Spirit has to divide here putting the spirit in charge to obey the Holy Spirit.

3. The soul-life clings to the innate possessions of earth. It loves material and physical things. Houses, lands, motor vehicles, clothing, toys, businesses, furniture, whatever. This is the part within us that is connected with self-interests, the natural instinct to self-preservation, and self-grasping of goods. Immediately as Light is shared, the soul love of possessions is put to the sword. Lot's wife turned back to "things" she didn't want to leave. Choices are made daily between renouncing this soul-tie to possessions or giving them over to the Lord. The undue absorption of the children of God with this aspect of the soul that denies its spirit to obey the Holy Spirit by an over-occupation with the affairs of this world, needs the knife of the Spirit.

4. Soulish self-love is another area (John 12:25) which means eternal loss because it proceeds from the first Adam. This grasping to "me" is manifested through the personality of the soul not brought into submission to the Holy One. "Is it a sin to keep it?" you ask. Yes, when the Light shines in and you see Truth. This is the place where the will of the believer must be set to be on God's side no matter what death occurs in its soul. The very will (choice maker) of the soul bows before its human spirit, abdicating the old Adam afresh so the new Adam might come forth.

When you are able to minister deliverance to believers who have left God's will and ways, part of that will be this breaking of the soul-ties and allowing the Holy Spirit access to move in the renewed spirit. Counselors, as you minister the grace of God in His name, maintain this centering in His only Son, Jesus Christ as True Lord and as the only Light able to dispel the forces of darkness for the long-term.

Let us now begin to expand our knowledge of religious sects and how they hinder the flow of the human spirit to live in obedience and harmony with the Father.

What is Religion?

Concerning the attacks and assaults against our spirit, further understanding must be had of what "religion" is. Vain religion is mankind trying to reach upward to God through every human method possible. Pagan nations are filled with this effort.

In much contrast to vain religion is born-again Christianity that begins with God reaching outward to humankind through the finished, satisfactory work of His only begotten Son Jesus, the Christ. God initiates this transaction, not humankind. It is a gift received by the utmost belief (faith) in Truth.

Salvation is free and freely given but it is not cheap, and believers give life-long effort to being conformed to the image of God's Son as a joyful and blessed renewing consequence that can never be earned with good works or by insincere confessions.

The one test that separates Christianity from all other religions, cults, sects, and philosophical ideologies, is the doctrine of the Trinity: God the Father, God the Son, God the Holy Spirit as One God. Christians are the only ones who believe in the Triune nature of God.

Attack by evil spirits against the human spirit, if allowed, soon becomes a stronghold of Satan working inside to destroy the very citadel of the Lord. Sins in the spirit are particularly repugnant because they interfere with and hinder our closest relationship with our Spiritual Father and delay or pervert the formation of the mind of Christ within.

SECTION I— What Is False Teaching And Unbelief?

Spiritual ignorance which sets the stage for unbelief is a primary and essential condition in a victim in order for deception by evil spirits to occur. Unbelief is the thief of victories won through believing prayer. Unbelief blinds us to the true causes of life's troubles. It hinders a clear vision of who Jesus Christ is as the consistant and faithful Healer, Deliverer, Provider, Strong Help, Savior, and Advocate He is on behalf of His children.

In short, people who are deceived and willfully remain so are in a state of unbelief under false teaching that reinforces deception in God's revealed Word. In this state they can never come into the victorious, peaceful and guilt-free life God intends for them until the light of the Lord breaks through this sin against the human spirit. Often, they do not even know how to recognize what false teaching is and how to be free of it.

The main characteristic in those who teach false doctrine is in falling short of *qualifying as righteous teachers.* According to God's revealed will righteous teachers are born anew in their spirits, annointed of God (Holy Spirit-led), and called to the ministry by the Lord then ordained to the teaching ministry—often by a local body of believers as in early church times. False teachers may have great followings. But that does not mean the true Church is growing, that Eternal God is worshipped, or that they are annointed of the Lord. Beware of the broad way and the flashy road signs of false teaching.

Other signs of righteous teachers (in contrast to false ones), are seen by their persistence to present the straight and narrow road to the Lord. They possess a personal maturity in the Lord and recognize the ways of the world. They have total, unqualified doctrinal agreement with the Word and maintain an attitude to spiritually guard and protect those for whom they are called by teaching Truth and not a lie (1 Tim 3:1-7, Ti 1:5-7, 1 Pe 5:1-4). True, godly teachers unveil Christ to their hearers and cause the Church to grow and flourish in righteousness (Eph 4:12-13).

Second Peter 2:1-21 describes false teachers as "..there will be false teachers among you. They will secretly introduce destructive heresies, even denying the sovereign Lord who bought them...Many will follow their shameful ways and will bring the way of truth into disrepute. In their greed these teachers will exploit you with stories they have made up. Their condemnation has long been hanging over them, and their destruction has not been sleeping..

Verse 6 continues with "..they are ungodly, (v10) despise authority, bold and arrogant, slander celestial beings; (v12) blaspheme in matters they do not understand; (v13) they will be paid back harm for the harm they have done; (v14) they seduce the unstable, are experts in greed; (v15) have left the straight way and wandered off to follow the way of Balaam; (v17) ..are springs without water and mists driven by a storm; (v18) they mouth empty, boastful words, and by appealing to the lustful desires of sinful human nature, they entice people who are just escaping from those who live in error... (v19) They promise them freedom, while they themselves are slaves of depravity—for a man is a slave to whatever has mastered him...

Then in verse 20 "..they are worse off at the end than they were at the beginning and (v21) it would have been better for them not to have known the way of righteousness, than to have known it and then to turn their backs on the sacred command that was passed on to them."

NOTICE THAT FALSE TEACHERS ONCE KNEW THE TRUTH AND BELIEVED THEMSELVES TO BE CHRISTIANS WITH A MESSAGE FROM GOD. HOWEVER, THEY ARE NOW DECEIVED AND ESPOUSING THE DOCTRINES OF DEMONS. THEIR TEACHING BRINGS DEATH.

False teachers bear poisonous fruit. Jesus said in Matthew 7:15-20 to *"watch out for false prophets. They come to you in sheep's clothing, but inwardly they are ferocious wolves. By their fruit* ('inward character' see Gal 5:22-25 for Fruit of the Spirit) *..you will recognize them. Do people pick grapes from thornbushes, or figs from thistles? Likewise, every good tree bears good fruit, but a bad tree bears bad fruit. A good tree cannot bear bad fruit, and a bad tree cannot bear good fruit."*

False teachers cause others to worship at the feet of idols (and many times, they are the idols). Deuteronomy 11:16, 27 warns to *"Be careful, or you will be enticed to turn away and worship other gods and bow down to them. Then the Lord's anger will burn against you, and he will shut the heavens so that it will not rain and the ground will yield no produce, and you will soon perish from the good land the Lord is giving you."*

WE ARE OPEN TO DECEPTION ONLY TO THE EXTENT THAT WE INSIST ON WALKING IN OUR OWN WAY OR HAR-BORING UNCONFESSED SIN. FALSE TEACHERS MUST BE EXPOSED AS AGENTS OF SATAN. COME YE OUT AND BE CLEAN OF THEM.

First Timothy 4:1 shows us that false teachers are imbued with the ideas, teachings, and satanic creed he wants proclaimed. These teachers—in our own time as the last days—will woo ungrounded believers away from the truth of Scripture. Listen to what it says: *"Now the Spirit speaketh expressly that in the latter times some shall depart from the faith, giving heed to SEDUCING SPIRITS and DOCTRINES OF DEVILS."*

Other Scriptures on False Teachers: 2 Cor 4:4 and 6:17; 1 John 2:9-11; Hos 4:12; Dt 11:27; 2 Jn 7; Rev 12:9, 20:8-10; 1 Tim 4:1; 1 Cor 3:14, 18.

Deceptions In Today's Church

Doctrinal deceptions that are taught by false teachers are basically derived from evil spirits fostering Satan's doctrines. He will use human sources that are sincerely deceived or who willingly practice error for some personal greed or impure motive.

What are the results of these evil teachers and evil doctrines against the believer? And further than that, against the world system we must live in before we are taken home? Listed in this section are some errors which have circulated in the Body caused by human or demon influence and control (Is 5:20). There may possibly be many more as the times are shortened.

What makes them so insidious? It is their attack against the human spirit as the head of the tripartite being in order to supplant the Holy Spirit's direction and break off Godly communication. An excellent booklet by John Ankerberg and John Weldon, "The Facts on False Teaching in the Church" is recommended reading on these cults.

1. TRIALS AND TRIBULATIONS DOCTRINE.
It is deception to believe that all negative or "bad" experiences (sickness, rejection, trials, financial loss, testing, disaster, family death, imprisonment) only come from Satan. It sounds good but shields the believer from reality and refutes what God says in Job 2:3-10: "Shall we accept (only) good at the hand of God and shall we not accept (also) misfortune and what is of a bad nature?"

In the trials (growth periods) of life, we need to be able to recognize what God is dealing with in us. Blaming everything on Satan causes us to miss what God has for us. The Word commands us to "count it all joy when trials and temptations befall you", because as we learn to listen to God in them we will mature in our faith (James 2).

God's children are rewarded for their suffering in the faith. We are to expect these natural, negative responses from living in a wicked world or as a consequence of deliberate sin on our part (Hebrews 12:4-12). Even Jesus Himself said in Matthew 25:37-46 that Christians can expect to be hungry, thirsty, strangers, naked needing clothing, ill in body, and imprisoned. This is the Cross-way, the path outlined for the overcomer.

2. SECULAR HUMANISM.
This is the world's attempt to enthrone human wisdom and morality as god, displacing the God of the universe and His way. In effect, Humanism is used for becoming a god (the last authority) in society. This intellectual soulish doctrine slips into churches and is rampant in many public schools as a "professional and ethical" way to properly socialize our nation. Its purpose is to make people "good".

In the local church Secular Humanism has crept in by placing less emphasis on the Word as inerrant and more emphasis on "Christian" entertainment or on social goodness programs. These churches experience little, if any, real worship of the Lord but have "a form of godliness, (yet) deny the power of God". The Cross of Christ is distinctly absent and

Biblical concepts such as repentance, sin nature, and eternal judgment are missing or redefined.

Humanism-oriented churches, denominations, and even ministries, often become wealthy and world-like with great social, athletic, and entertainment complexes. Instead of houses of prayer and powerhouses for reaching the lost, they are humanistic.

Secular Humanism espouses situation ethics, "doing what is right for you", and "the end is worth the means" (Hitler believed that!) or, "war is alright...it will boost the economy" philosophies. Twentieth century citizens have seen great loads of food, clothing, and aid sent in response to third world pleas. This may or may not be sound political sense for a nation. However, TO THE CHRISTIAN, our Lord's commission is to:

"..Go into all the world AND PREACH THE GOOD NEWS TO ALL CREATION..Whoever believes and is baptized will be saved, but whoever does not believe will be condemned. And these signs will accompany those who believe, IN MY NAME they will drive out demons, they will speak in new tongues, they will pick up snakes with their hands, and when they drink deadly poison, it will not hurt them at all; they will place their hands on sick people, and they will get well." (Mk 16:15-18).

Humanism perverts and counterfeits the commission of Christ by bringing temporary changes to physical needs but no eternal change to the spirit and soul. For Christians, proper response to human, physical need comes out of an apostolic foundation of evangelism to the lost first and a helping hand to fellow believers in need as the Scriptures admonish. It does not come from vain and worldly "do-good gestures" that comfortably slip people into hell.

3. POSITIVE CONFESSION AND DEMAND HEALING. There is a demand belief in "health and wealth" doctrines that smack of witchcraft, is presumptious, and testing of God. People will say the following things in the name of positive confession: "I WILL receive my $4 million—it is my right as a child of God". Or, "I speak the word of faith to claim what I feel as a king's kid, I am deserving of.." They might even threaten God with "If You don't answer my prayer of positive confession and heal me (send money, get me a job, bring me a wife, etc., etc.), I'll fast until I die." Unfortunately, people have actually died waiting on their "claim of faith" to work for them.

You can see how ridiculous, manipulative, and fanatical this perverted "positive confession" can become in someone not grounded in the Word and in those who do not know God or His character as One who delights in giving to His children WHAT IS GOOD FOR THEM. We need not stamp our feet at God and insist on our way because we've said the "magic words" or fantasized something different for where we are or where we want to be. Conversely, faith always agrees with the Word of God no matter what it says. And it may say we are to give the widow's mite.

Think on this: our Lord is to be held in awe and reverance. He is Sovereign and our will (soul) cannot override His. God has given us wills to choose right or wrong but they are not divine and certainly are not more powerful that the mightly plan of God which takes into consideration the whole world through all ages, before, during, and after Time, into eternity. Submission to His will is walking humbly before the Lord.

4. PSYCHOLOGY: TODAY'S WORLDLY WISDOM. This is another counterfeit and perversion of Godly wisdom seen in trying to fit the world's philosophy (at best, using God's methods without having God) into the Christian lifestyle. Sometimes it is not a perversion but a radical substitution. As a deception, it makes sense and easily appeals to some Christians as "learning faith-producing techniques" or for gaining "spiritual power, health, wealth, etc. with God".

Just what is psychology, anyway? Briefly it is the study of why people are the way they are and how they can change by behavior modification in any of some 10,000 ways. The secular world, however, does not recognize the One God we know yet calls their god(s) "the universal mind", "nature", "the force", "the collective unconscious" or "individuation". These are not just other names for God but substitutes for God.

What followed along the paths of ancient spiritism in the early Nineteenth Century onward was the creation of psychoanalysis by Sigmund Freud, Eric Fromm, and Carl Jung. Each laid a strong intellectual base for the introduction and integration of "science" with religion and the occult. It will become even more developed into the Twenty-first Century by New Age teaching, and by hundreds of psychologists who have added to this body of knowledge through "pop psychology" paperback books.

Ancient sorcery employed mind-over-matter philosophies that have been revived today and seem to work (for a season). These are devastatingly changing the worldview by claiming to create mind-links across continents and are increasingly identified with occultic powers. But the Lord tells us *"the things to which the Gentiles (pagans) sacrifice, they sacrifice to demons, AND NOT TO GOD; and I do not want you to become sharers in demons"* (1 Cor 10:20).

PSYCHOLOGY WILL "SCIENTIFICALLY" IDENTIFY DE-MONS. IT WILL THEN TRAIN YOU TO LIVE WITH THEM THE BEST WAY POSSIBLE — BUT AT GREAT COST.

Don't be misled by "christian psychology", a contradiction in terms. Since the psyche is the soul, we can either operate out of the soul-life (flesh) or from the renewed human spirit which is in direct contact with the Holy Spirit and directed by the Lord. A pure vessel does not operate from both (James 3:13-18).

Take Schuller's popular "christian" philosophy of "Possibility Thinking". It is one such teaching that uses meditation as a launching pad (PTM) making the human attitude responsible to change the person into something better. This brand of psychology falsely appears as "self-improvement for the realization of full human potential". How much strengthening of the soulish life is needed to walk as a Christian? You are right, none. The cross-life is what is needed to assist the human spirit find and follow God's way.

On the other hand Christian counseling is an opportunity to reveal God's wisdom and plan solely from a Scriptural basis to fellow believers. When this divine source of wisdom was usurped from pastors, priests, and brothers and sisters in the faith by worldly, professional psychologists (with their State-approved licenses to earn a living thereby) the Church lost a great deal.

Sadly, some Christian parents are fearful today to guide, discipline, and instruct their own children preferring or indoctrinated to leaving these responsibilities and blessings of parenthood to "specialists" in child psychology. There is no specialist more expert to help you and your family than God Himself. He uses His Word to do it and His annointed ones.

Seeking power over your position in the world from within the soulish intellect is contrary to God's divine order. Realize and be thankful that He has complete control. Do not fear but trust and allow Him to have His control because no amount of "trying to understand yourself to get out of it" will succeed. It is sin against your own spirit and certainly insulting to the Lord.

Chapter 5

How Can Unforgiveness Withhold Spiritual Health?

One key to a positive, victorious, demon vexation-free life is found in taking up your cross in forgiving men and women their sins against you. Unforgiveness is idolatry. Why is this so? Because it enthrones—as an idol—bitterness, hurts, hatred, and anger against an offender instead of giving them up to God to deal with. Most of the problems people face right now involve the unforgiveness of others, themselves, or an unforgiving attitude against God.

Think about it.

Counselors, slow down as you read this section to allow God to bring into your own minds those for whom you have negative feelings and anger. As you go through this exercise, you will be enabled to take the counselee step-by-step through the forgiveness process.

Again, stop to listen as He tells you who you have any bitterness, hatred, grudges against, or ill will toward. Bitterness is the mature offspring of decayed hurts in your spirit and soul that are kept alive by constant remembrance either by thinking silently on them or speaking them aloud.

Bitterness results in an unwillingness to either release yourself from its torment or rebellion against God who, you feel, doesn't understand how hurt you are or who "allowed it to happen to you". Unforgiveness can also stem from the evil desire to continue to somehow "punish" the offender. It is born of hate and defiles the spirit to the point of infecting the soul-life with weak and unhealthy human interaction so that Christian help is not sought. The body also is exposed to disease from fostering bitterness.

Act against this force by willing yourself to forgive the Lord, yourself, and others. This is a crucial point of victory in all deliverance. Everything stops in a person's deliverance when unforgiveness is harbored. In fact, such a one is not Scripturally allowed to partake of the Lord's table without first getting your heart right with Him and others. If you have taken the Eucharist with unforgiveness, you must apologize to God for that and make it right between yourself and Him.

> *"Whoever eats the bread or drinks the cup of the Lord in an unworthy manner will be guilty of sinning against the body and blood of the Lord. A man ought to examine himself before he eats of the bread and drinks of the cup. FOR ANYONE WHO EATS AND DRINKS WITHOUT RECOGNIZING THE BODY OF THE LORD eats and drinks judgment on himself. That is why many among you are weak and sick, and a number of you have fallen asleep..."* 1 Cor 11:27-33.

"And when ye stand praying FORGIVE, IF YOU HAVE AUGHT AGAINST ANY: that your Father also which is in heaven may forgive you YOUR trespasses. But IF YOU DO NOT FORGIVE, NEITHER WILL YOUR FATHER WHICH IS IN HEAVEN FORGIVE YOU." Mk 11:25-26 (KJV).

Barriers of Unforgiveness

Many Christians fortify and maintain the barriers they make around themselves so tightly, God Himself is blocked. This kind of fear and unwillingness to allow God access gives Satan a legal claim on their lives to rob it of fulfillment, of a love for life, of freedom from fear, and sometimes of physical health, satisfaction, and a true peace with God and man. Remember, Satan is a lion seeking the wounded whom he can kill and devour. He knows full well how to get at your weakest place that is so well guarded.

Refusing to forgive and retain bitterness can result in:
1. Physical fatigue and loss of sleep, sickness, worry.
2. An inability to love God fully: by extention, love others and be a loving personality.
3. Depression arising from an insecure position.
4. Bitterness passed from generation to generation (feuds).
5. Binding others from receiving God's redemptive workings
"Whosesoever sins ye remit, they are remitted unto them; and whosesoever sins ye retain, they are retained" (Jn 20:23).
6. A judging spirit (Mt 7:2, Ro 2:1).
7. A troubled life for self and others (Heb 12:14-15).

And may I tell you in all love that God allows very harsh things to come into your life to bring any hard core of unforgiveness to the Light. The seven results of bitterness just listed may be the loving fingers of Father reaching into your life in a way you can understand for by them you do realize something is very definitely wrong, correct? This is God's order to heal your spirit of them and bring lasting freedom.

When Satan's works come to the light, people are set free of his snare but also set into a life of blessing. Now, you may experience pain at so bright and Holy a light piercing your innerman, but the joy of liberty is well worth the momentary pain of facing self and allowing the Light become the norm for you. So why not release your unforgiveness to the Light of God for cleansing of those dark, dank corners?

Forgiving from your heart is not an option to the Christian. It is essential to understanding the nature of God. Forgiving gets you in step with Him and allows you to be forgiven BY Him on a constant basis. Forgiving yourself, others, and the Lord frees you from guilt. It releases the destructive bitterness waging war in your spirit, soul, and body. It allows you to finally see YOUR OWN offense before God in continuing to react to others' sinning against you by taking it out on yourself and on them.

Counselors, as an aid to helping you release forgiveness in yourself and while assisting the counselee, this simple confession is given here. Sincere words of confession must be spoken even if you don't "feel" anything. This acts to verbally state your intention of forgiving. God does not want you to justify yourself or put the blame on others—that smokescreen is not in the confession. It is simple. So you be simple. Be sincere. Take some time by naming names and make it a decision of your will.

"I WAS WRONG TO SIN AGAINST_____
BY MY REBELLIOUS ATTITUDE OF UNFORGIVENESS.
DEAR GOD, PLEASE FORGIVE ME AS I FORGIVE
_____."

I trust you have forgiven everyone possible you can even think of. The Lord may bring others to mind in the coming weeks—just go ahead and forgive them quickly when He does because forgiveness is an ongoing process as the Light shines in.

The second step in forgiving is to RELEASE THEM (Mt 18:27) which cancels their spiritual debt against you and extends your mercy toward them (1 Pe 2:1). This is the glorious part where forgeting the sin is possible. "Cancel" means you choose not to harbor any hurtful feelings, intentions, thoughts,or actions against them JUST AS YOUR HEAVENLY FATHER HAS CANCELLED YOUR DEBTS AND TRESPASSES.

It is highly probable—SO BE AWARE—that Satan will attempt to bring new thoughts of old bitternesses or hatreds back into your mind. When this happens, you remind him that on today's date you forgave that person. Tell him to leave you alone in the Name of Jesus Christ because all that sin is now under the Blood of Christ and cancelled!

Do not for one moment coddle the accusations of Satan regarding unforgiveness. You must overcome in this area and by God's grace, you will. As time passes and your mind continues to be renewed by this obedience to the Lord the attacks will cease altogether. It is at that stage that you will have truly forgotten the incident and be totally healed. Just keep short accounts, don't hold grudges, and keep on forgiving others whether they deserve it or not. The important thing is that you deserve to be free and remain free.

Other Scriptures Regarding Forgiveness: Eph 4:31-32; Matthew 5:22-24, 6:12-15, 18:21-22, 34-35; Is 43:18, Ps 18:25, Lk 6:36, Col 3:12-13, Gal 5:15, 2 Cor 2:10-11, Ro 14:4,10, and Ac 8:23.

SECTION II—The Occult And Witchcraft

More than any other involvement in Satan's domain, the occult is the most obvious and also the most insidious in its quest to detach the believer's spirit from God's Spirit. Being naturally curious, humans gravitate to the unknown, to powers and powerful ones, to understanding the who, when, why, where, and how a thing operates.

God the Father has provided us with ample information on the wiles and operations of the devil in His Word. THAT is where we find out about them, not from sorcerers, witches, clairvoyants, cults, occult literature, fortune readings, astrologists, seances, mental attitude books, satan worship, and the like (See Appendix III). Indeed, God's Word tells us what the occult is, how to avoid it, and how to overcome Satan's attempts, attacks, and open prostitution of our spirits by seduction to himself and his dark kingdom.

It is in the arena of our spirit that we must prove loyal, stedfast, and faithful to the God who loves us now and who literally gave His very life to redeem us from the curse sin brings. The occult is a constant battle that changes face and intensity as we are exposed to the new and unusual that is constantly bombarded on us Christians through television, books, movies, magazines, music, trends and styles, and "intellectual thought".

I want to emphasize something regarding the protection of children from Christian homes. Very special attention must be given to the schools they are placed in, to the teachers they get, to the newest toys, games, computer programs, clothing, music, and to drug availability. Our children are exposed to making bad choices in companions and living in a perilous environment that continually draws it away from God in order to be obedient to present governing authorities.

Educate yourself and your family about the forms the occult takes so that by a united family resistance, strength and support will uphold and maintain all of you and not be used to tear the family apart. Join together to cleanse your home and possessions of all occult influences—destroying them, not simply throwing them out.

Spiritual warfare is the task of each family member. It has proven to be a positive step for children to take part in cleaning out their own rooms of books, comics, tapes, records, posters, clothing, toys, computer games, T-shirts, and anything else occult they possess. People have told me that their children began to realize their own authority to resist the devil and destroy his power and influence over them by their active participation. The children were consequently able to find peace in their rooms instead of unease and distraction. Children need quiet time, too.

How Do We Make A Positive Rejection Of The Occult?

First, REPENT. You must ask God's forgiveness for going after foreign gods, idols, and demons (in occultic forms) and believe that He has forgiven you.

The second thing to do is RENOUNCE your previous and present involvement in them OUT LOUD by naming each trespass individually. To renounce means "to turn away, turn your back on, forsake, reject, deny, dismiss, drive away, cease from, depart from, separate, a reversal, disown, to speak or say "off", bid, call, and command to go."

Renouncing is an act of your will in obedience to your spirit following God's Holy Spirit. It is a choice you make to go God's revealed way and not another's way. It has nothing to do with feelings. It is a cold decision to cut yourself loose from all power of the enemy in, over, and through your life.

Renouncing the occult removes the LEGAL, AUTHORIZED RIGHT of Satan in your spirit and frees your spirit to commune WITHOUT FILTHINESS with God the Father, Son, and Holy Spirit. The Lord is calling you to holiness and godliness and wishes you to come up higher with Him in sweet communion.

After deliverance of the occult, THE CONFESSON OF VICTORY is helpful as a third step to clarify your Biblical position (See Appendix I) and reinforce by Scripture your spirit's stand and holy position.

"When you enter the land the Lord your God is giving you, do not learn to imitate the detestable ways of the nations there. Let no one be found among you who sacrifices his son or daughter in the fire, who practices divination or sorcery, interprets omens, engages in

witchcraft, or casts spells, or who is a medium or spiritist or who consults the dead. Anyone who does these things is detestable to the Lord, and because of these detestable practices, the Lord your God will drive out those nations before you. YOU MUST BE BLAMELESS BEFORE THE LORD YOUR GOD." Dt 18:9-13.

"Joshua said to the people, 'You are not able to serve the Lord. He is a holy God; he is a jealous God. He will not forgive your rebellion and your sins. If you forsake the Lord and serve foreign gods, he will turn and bring disaster on you and make an end of you after he has been good to you.' BUT the people said to Joshua, 'NO, WE WILL SERVE THE LORD.' 'Now then', said Joshua, 'THROW AWAY THE FOREIGN GODS THAT ARE AMONG YOU and yield your hearts to the Lord'..." Jos 24:19-23.

"Can your idols make such claims as these? Let them come and show what they can do, says God, the King of Israel. Let them try to tell us what occurred in years gone by, or what the future holds. Yes, that's it! If you are gods, tell what will happen in the days ahead! Or by some mighty miracle that makes us stare, amazed. But no! You are LESS THAN NOTHING AND CAN DO NOTHING AT ALL. Anyone who chooses you, needs his head examined!" Is 41:21-24 (LIV).

NOTE: an idol is anything at all—physical, mental, ambitions, money, etc. that replaces the Lord as the UPPERMOST in importance and position in your life. What ungodly things do you give most attention and regard to? Your money and love to? Those are the idols.

"No one can serve two masters. Either he will hate the one and love the other, or he will be devoted to the one and despise the other. You cannot serve both God and Money." Mt 6:22-24.

"Regard not them that have familiar spirits, neither seek after wizards, to be defiled by them. I am the Lord your God." Lev 19:31 (KJV).

"The images of their gods you are to burn in the fire. Do not covet the silver and gold on them, and do not take it for yourselves, or you will be ensnared by it, for it is detestable to the Lord your God. Do not bring a detestable thing into your house or you, like it, will be set

apart for destruction. UTTERLY ABHORE AND DETEST IT, FOR IT IS SET APART FOR DESTRUCTION.'' Dt 7:25-26.

This chapter has been filled with the will of God. Every Scripture is His will. Now the obedience of the known will of God rests on you in your heart of hearts. Pull down those idols attacking your spirit in the high places that the Lord faithfully reveals to you. Be steadfast in becoming free. Our next move is into the attacks against the soul, the topic of Chapter Six.

CHAPTER 6

The Attack Against
The Human Soul

SECTION I— Moving From Curse To Blessing

Every person who has ever been born from Adam and Eve's children forward were born under the CURSE of sin. This inborn sin the Jews called iniquity has within it the seed of rebellion against God, the Creator. Unfortunately by its very nature and consequences, sin brings cursed living and physical death to all humans.

Fortunately, this very curse of sin had been taken by Jesus Christ when He died (Ro 6:23) so that those who choose Him as Savior are unloaded of sin and its bondage over them. By this holy transposition of sin onto the sinless One and off of the sin-filled ones, we are made capable of BLESSING.

Calvary was the unique act God demanded that a Divine Exchange could take place. In this way only, could humankind stand before Him as clean, acceptable, and under blessing (2 Cor 5:21). Christ calculatingly took the negative side of the curse along with its eternal separation from God. It happened the very moment Christ cried, "My God, my God, why have You forsaken Me?"

But redemption has two sides. Christ also gave the positive side of redemption to His children in healing of their sicknesses, righting their souls, and renewing their spirits (Is 53:4-5, 1 Pt 2:24, Mt 8:17). Jesus tasted death that we might share His eternal life (Heb 2:9). He took on Himself poverty that we might share His abundance (2 Cor 8:9). He was rejected of the Father that we might have acceptance (Mt 27:46). He became a curse for us that we might be free of all curses and be blessed (Gal 3:13-14, Dt 21:22-23). What a tremendous exchange!

Briefly, evil (curses) came upon Christ so that good (blessing) could come upon His children. What a wonder! What love! Derek Prince has a marvelous teaching on Blessings and Curses and his materials can be purchased directly from his organization at Post Office Box 300, Dept 88E, Ft. Lauderdale, Florida, 33303, USA.

How To Recognize Blessing And Curse

A CURSE is defined as a prayer or invocation to call up harm or injury; a prayer of evil, an oath, a cause of great evil: to swear profanely and invoke evil upon; blasphemy, to call upon divine or supernatural power(s) to send injury upon. SATAN IS THE POWERHOUSE OF CURSES. People representing Satan can curse others.

God is able to curse (Gen 12:3; 27:29) and will use this to protect His children, set limits for good and blessed living (by obeying or disobeying His commandments), and to meet His own purposes. Men of God can curse (Jos 6:26). Jesus spoke curses (Mk 11:20-21). Living under a curse is being the "tail" (Dt 28:13,44) and produces humiliation, failure to reproduce, sickness, family breakdown, poverty, defeat, oppression, disfunctional human relationships, physical hardship, and God's disfavor.

BLESSING is God's favor. It is health, having the Kingdom prosperity of peace, joy, love, and spiritual fruitfulness. Blessing is being reproductive in any area, living life without fear, having financial sufficiency (wealth and worldly success are not guaranteed); victory, long life, and natural happiness. Blessings proceed from God or those representing Him. You, as God's child, can bless others. SATAN CANNOT BLESS, ONLY CURSE.

Once a curse or a blessing is released in the form of words—verbal, written, or by thoughts—they tend to go on through time (up to the third and fourth generations) until revoked . It is possible, therefore, for things to happen in your life which were originally set in motion in previous generations. Living under the blessing of God is being the "head" (Dt 28:13,44) and is the normal Christian life. No Christian need live under any curse for they are not the heritage of the Lord and can be prayfully broken by the power of Jesus Christ.

A List of Common Curse Indications

1. Mental and/or emotional breakdown; mental disease.

2. Repeated or chronic sicknesses, especially if hereditary or without clear diagnosis and treatment.

3. Repeated miscarriages or related female problems; impotency.

4. The breakdown of marriage; family alienation where the family literally falls apart; repeated divorces.

5. Continuing financial insufficiency; especially where income appears to be sufficient. A little with God's blessing does more than a lot with a curse attached to it.

6. In a family or nation, a history of suicide or unnatural death, terrorism, serial murders, economic failure, overthrow and revolution.

The Primary Cause For Living Under Blessing Or Curses

Deuteronomy 28:1-2 admonishes us to *"..FULLY OBEY the Lord your God and CAREFULLY FOLLOW all his commands I give you today, (then) the Lord your God will set you high above all the nations on earth. All these blessings will come upon you and accompany you if you OBEY the Lord your God."* (Read the long list of blessings given in this passage).

Deuteronomy 28:15 begins with a warning *"However, if you DO NOT OBEY the Lord your God and DO NOT CAREFULLY FOLLOW ALL his commands and decrees I am giving you today, all these curses will come upon you and overtake you."* (Read the list of curses and their consequences in this passage).

BLESSINGS ARISE BECAUSE A PERSON:
#1 LISTENS TO THE VOICE OF THE LORD and
#2 OBEYS THAT WORD OF THE LORD TO THEM.
Blessing comes out of a relationship with God.

CURSES ARISE BECAUSE A PERSON:
#1 DOES NOT LISTEN TO THE VOICE OF THE LORD and
#2 DISOBEYS GOD'S COMMANDS TO THEM.
A faulty or nonexistent relationship with God brings curses.

Secondary causes for living under curses are found in Exodus 20:3-6 and may be summarized as follows:

1. Practicing idolatry, having or tolerating false gods or the occult (same as worshipping false gods).

2. Dishonoring parents. A person with wrong attitudes toward their par-

ents will never come under the blessing of God.

3. Illicit or unnatural sex including adultery, fornication, incest, homosexuality, sodomy, bestiality (sex with animals), pornography, sex with or against children.

4. Injustice to the weak or the helpless: the deliberate procurring of or assisting in abortions, euthanasia, cannibalizing the unborn or newborn for body parts to commercial or ungodly purposes.

5. Trusting in man (the arm of flesh, morality, education, cleverness, politicking); his programs or finance schemes for the love of money or power (Jer 17:5-6, Gal 3:1-14).

6. Stealing or by perjury under oath (Zec 5:1-4).

7. Deception (Mal 1:14; 3-8-10); promising to give something to God then drawing back (Ananias spirit Acts 5).

8. Parental or teachers' curses pronounced on children ("You'll never make good", "You are stupid, lazy, ugly, crazy..."). Children, and later as adults, can struggle for years under these verbal curses until they are broken.

9. Self-imposed curses: Rachel took Jacob's curse on herself (Gen 27:13, 46). We are to make positive confessions of the mouth (Ps 118:17)—not confess to stupidity, guilt, etc.

10. Curses pronounced by Satan's people against you, your household, race, gender or nation (Dt 23:4-5 Balaam).

11. Soulish prayers, complaints, gossip against yourself or others, murmuring (Ja 3:14-15). You can destroy people with your tongue (Jer 18:18).

12. Curses from joining unscriptual covenants(Ex 23:32) like Freemasonry, fraternities, sororities, false churches, street gangs, clans, cults. Joining them unites you with those who are on the side of evil forces alien to God.

Battling In The Heavenlies Releases Curses

To battle against the power of curses, however placed on us, we must move from the base of LEGAL STANDING gained in salvation through Christ's shed blood onward into the EXPERIENTIAL of willfully taking and appropriating God's provision of freedom. It includes these four steps for the Christian:

1. RECOGNIZE the true nature of your problem: when and where sin entered in. (In finances, for example, it might be as simple as never having given a regular and consistant amount of money to God (the Old Testament

tithe established a covenant relationship; offerings above that produced blessing (Mal 3:6-12) or the fact that your whole family line has been poverty stricken).

2. REPENT of whatever initially exposed you to the problem whether it was your own sin or the sin of ancestors. (Consulting a medium, a great-grandparent slave trader, or whatever sin you know to be against the direct will of God in your family.) You may wish to say, "Lord, please forgive me and any member of my family that participated in _____ " (See Appendix III).

3. RENOUNCE the curse with your mouth out loud: "This curse no longer belongs to me. I do not accept it. Through Jesus Christ I have the right to be free from it. It is not my problem any longer and is broken in my life and over my family in the name of Jesus, the only Christ."

4. RESIST by taking a definite and active stand against the power of Satan. Resisting the devil is one of the most definite things the Bible tells us to do. James 4:7 tells us to FIRST submit to God THEN resist the devil. The result is that he MUST FLEE. No one can resist the devil for you. It is a daily walk of faith and pinnacle where we see God at work on our behalf.

Eight Requirements For Revoking Curses

1. AS A CHRISTIAN your faith must be based on the Word of God (Gal 3:13-14, Ep 1:7, Col 1:13-14, 1 Jn 3:8, Lk 10:19).

2. CONFESS with your mouth your faith in Jesus Christ (Heb 3:1). If a confession out loud is not made, you do not release Christ to work supernaturally on your behalf. Confessing Christ as Lord and Savior places you firmly in God's camp.

3. COMMIT yourself to obedience. Blessings come to those who hear and obey. Releasing yourself to the grace of God enables you to commit yourself in faith to Him.

4. CONFESS ANY KNOWN SINS of your's or of your ancestors. You do not bear the guilt of their sin but you are bearing the consequences (Proverbs 28:13). If you cover sin you will not prosper (spirit of Sapphira Acts 5).

5. FORGIVE all other persons, organizations, and yourself (Mk 11:25). Mention them by name and forgive each one. Go back as far as necessary in memory to forgive all who have offended and been your enemy. If YOU want total forgiveness you must also GIVE it.

6. RENOUNCE all contact with the occult or secret societies you or your family have had. If you are still involved, quit them outright. Then get rid of ALL objects, symbols, or materials that have anything even remotely connected with them to the occult. They must be destroyed totally. To bring any accursed thing into your house brings the consequences of that curse upon you and your family. It is a familiar object.

7. RELEASE YOURSELF in the name of Jesus. Believe and read this out loud: *"Whoever calls on the name of the Lord will be saved; for on Mount Zion and in Jerusalem there will be deliverance among the survivors whom the Lord calls."* And *"I tell you the truth, whatever I bind on earth will be bound in heaven, and whatever I loose on earth will be loosed in heaven."* This is the spiritual authority needed to meet the conditions to loose yourself on earth which looses you in the heavenlies from any curse.

8. Finally, THANK AND PRAISE GOD for your deliverance from the effects and consequences of curses that have hung over you and your family. They are revoked. As God opens your mind to other areas repeat these steps until you, your family and home are clean. Never forget to rejoice and thank your Father.

SECTION II—Satan's Strongholds In The Soul
Rebellion And Its Roots

The importance of understanding the role of rebellion in deliverance is seen in Psalm 107:11-12 (LIV): *"They rebelled against the Lord, scorning Him who is the God above all gods. That is why He broke them with hard labor; they fell and none would help them rise again."* Rebellion cannot be healed. Rebellion must be broken.

To be rebellious is to take a position in opposition to the Lord's will by either not listening to Him or listening but not obeying what He has shown you to be righteous behavior. A toddler who challenges and rebels at her parents' desires for her good, indicates the attitude, if unbroken, she will carry into adulthood toward the heavenly Father. Rebellion compounds its strength if it is not broken and dealt with in its earliest stages.

Let's face it. Everyone knows when they are being contrary. They know when they are forcing their own ways and opinions, desires or control on others. It goes on in Christian fellowships, marriages and often is acted out against our heavenly Father. An intensity of rebellion against the Word of God causes suffering and demonic vexation within and without the personality.

Rebellion in the soul-life says, "I will have my own way no matter what the cost to myself or to you!" In your mind's eye, can you not see the "bratty child" within that adult standing there and insisting on their wishes, trying desparately to overcome all objections? But they will not be moved off their position of rebellion.

But praise God that as a loving Father He will not allow His headstrong, willful child rush over cliffs to self-destruction without attempting to redirect him or her to the peaceful path He has planned for that life. Conversely, Satan will jump on every opportunity left open by that strain of rebellion to keep him or her headed for the cliffs of destruction.

Rebellion against God has root causes in pride (I am sufficient to meet the needs and demands of life), in self-centeredness (I will do it myself, my way), in carnality (I will walk, dress, talk, live in the world's way), and in immovability through a wounded spirit (I will put up walls that no one—not even God—can surmount).

God's desire for His children is a broken spirit and a contrite heart that can quickly hear and obey Him without question or hesitation. This quickness of spirit comes with maturity and out of a profoundly deep love of the Lord God for Himself. There is much teaching from the Bible on the connection between rebellion and witchcraft, hearing God and obeying:

"Now, if you will fear and worship the Lord and LISTEN to his commandments and NOT REBEL against the Lord, and if..you follow the Lord your God, then all will be well. But if you rebel against the Lord's commandments and refuse to listen to him, then HIS HAND WILL BE AS HEAVY UPON YOU as it was upon your ancestors." 1 Sam 12:14.

"An evil man seeketh only rebellion: Therefore a cruel messenger shall be sent against him." Pr 17:11 (KJV).

"And the angel of the Lord said to him..Behold, I have come out as an adversary, because your way was contrary to me." Numbers 22:32 (NAS).

"And you (He made alive), when you were dead (slain) by (your) trespasses and sins in which at one time you walked habitually. You were following the course and fashion of this world…were under the sway of the tendency of this present age…following the prince of the power of the air. (You were obedient to him and were under his control) the (demon) spirit that still constantly works in the sons of DIS-OBEDIENCE, the CARELESS, the REBELLIOUS and the UNBELIEVING who go against the purposes of God." Ep 2:1-2 (AMP).

"For REBELLION IS AS THE SIN OF WITCHCRAFT, and stubbornness is as iniquity and idolatry. Because thou hast rejected the word of the Lord, He hath also rejected thee…" 1 Sam 15:23 (KJV).

The Jezebel Spirit is a Root

God is Order and has clearly set boundaries for his earth, in the animal and plant kingdoms, and for humankind. He has unmistakable bench-marks regarding authority and submission, higher and lower, holy and un-clean. A perversion of God's order is chronicled in 1 Kings 16-21 in the history of King Ahab and his wife, Jezebel who both confused the authori-ty and order of male and female as God ordained. This is the first identity of the Jezebel spirit.

New Testament writings continue to uphold male leadership and spiritual authority in the local church. Both men and women may have leadership positions, be called as apostles, prophets, missionaries, and teachers but they are positioned there by others in higher authority. Godly order demands a submission to those who have the rule over the flock and will not seek to steal that authority for themselves by their own will and scheme.

The Jezebel spirit gains control in two ways. First, using the 1 Kings sto-ry as an example, King Ahab GAVE AWAY his authority by allowing Jeze-bel to usurp it (to confiscate, steal away by force without legal right). And secondly, Jezebel TOOK IT for her own purposes. So we see a giving up on the part of one person and a taking over on the part of the second person. A Jezebel spirit cannot steal a ministry or trip up a man of God: this posi-tion is either willfully and/or passively given over.

Jezebel used and perverted her husband's ordained, kingly authority as a force to destroy Elijah the Prophet of God. She was a pagan who did not like God's message, wanted to remain in her rebellion and maliciously with evil intent, pursued the bringing down of God's authority and voice to His people in Elijah. This is how the jezebel spirit tries to destroy servants of God (those in the ministry operating in the gifts and calling of God).

The Philistine Jezebel was the high priestess of Baal and intent on subverting the Hebrew ways of Ahab into Satanic rites. She used cunning, sweet words, the most subtle manners to outright deceit, hatred, rebellion, murder, fear, and governing authority. She mobilized hundreds of false prophets to bring down Elijah. It was a desperate situation for the Prophet of God who was so overcome with fear that he errantly ran from God (though it looked to Elijah like he was running from Jezebel), forfeited his holy prophet's calling and became spiritually impotent in the face of the jezebel spirit operating within Jezebel, the woman.

This same spirit is mentioned in the New Testament:

"..Nevertheless, I have this against you: You tolerate that woman Jezebel who calls herself a prophetess. By her teaching she misleads my servants into sexual immorality and the eating of food sacrificed to idols...and I will make those who commit adultery with her suffer intensely, unless they repent of her ways. I will strike her children dead..." Rev 2:18-23.

While the Jezebel spirit goes after the prophets (the mouth of God) first, they will then seek out the most Godly intercessors to deceive (the warriors of God) and if not dealt with there, will go after the pastors (the overseers of the flock) next.

Often you will find these people in the Bible studies, worship and music areas, in leadership positions or close to those who are leaders, appearing as humble Christian servants. Their objective, either known or unknown to them, is to subvert the Word of God by false teaching, promote Satan's kingdom from within, and spiritually cripple the people of God. They bring confusion, uneasiness, false tales, and pseudo-prophecies using political maneuvering to cause discord and splits within the body.

Jezebel is the spiritual spawner of all who pursue libertine doctrines and practices wishing to usurp the authority of God in the Church by replacing it with doctrines of demons. Males or females can have a jezebel spirit. Counselors will encounter them and must remember that these are people caught in the sticky web of Satan needing to be illuminated of their precarious position and given opportunity for repentance and deliverance.

Thankfully, the church is emplowered to overthrow the spirits of Jezebel (the aggressor) and Ahab (the compliant) in their congregations by recognizing and dealing with them through the spiritual warfare of intercessory prayer. Should these people remain unwilling to deal with the sin of harboring these spirits which cause the Body so many problems, a confrontation by the pastor with his vestry, elders, or deacons is necessary. If they refuse help that is offered, outright dismissal in church discipline may be called for (1 Tim 4:1-7; Matthew 18:15-19).

Pride And Self-Centered Living

No amount or quality of exposure or involvement in Christian living, teaching, counselling, ministry, spiritual service, and good works is effective in the one who resists a complete surrender of his or her will to God for His use. Jesus Christ is Lord (owner, chief, boss, controller) of your life or you are continuing in your own pride and self-centered habits.

A prideful person is centered on life benefitting him or her and is selfish (thinks of self first, last, always). Generally, the more easily offended and hurt a person is, the more pride-filled they are. People who are dead to their first Adam life are not hurt: they are dead. It is a historical fact in nations that pride can be so strong over losing face in a situation that suicide is contemplated and often accomplished (especially oriental and indian societies). Pride is a tenacious and destructive root.

When one feels empty, threatened, insecure or dejected, pride raises its head in false comfort. It will attempt to justify the inadequate feelings by putting these thoughts into the mind of the hurt one. It will reason: "I wasn't 100% wrong!" and, "I'm tough enough to handle this alone." Or, "Look at them—what right do THEY have to criticize ME?". Pride comforts the soul by attempting to bring down the "offender" to a level of guilt actually brought on by the pride-filled person.

Christ's way is humility. Humility is the opposite of pride. A humble person quickly gives in, does not assert himself but reflects the very nature of the Lord. It is a fruit of the Spirit and goes hand-in-glove with wholeness, harmony, and order. It seeks nothing for itself and is not easily offended.

Look at pride in the form of self-centeredness. This attitude upsets unity from the sandbox to the corporate boardroom to the marriage bed. Pride in one's self neutralizes the release of God's power to right a situation. It undermines faith and begets the sin of unbelief. Pride is fashioned on exalted misconceptions and shadowy pretexts. Satanic truth says that a person can become a god and pride buys into that error. Snap! the trap shuts.

As pride strengthens itself from situation to situation, soul-dominance develops to continually assert itself to lead and not submit to the spirit. Pride is a huge door for Satan to enter and is often the strongman in many people's lives. After all, pride caused Lucifer's great fall (Is 14:12-17) and is the antipathy to Jesus Christ's humility.

The lust of money often expressed by gambling or hoarding is a selfishness that will steal from a blessed life of providing for one's own family and others. Again, either Jesus Christ is Lord of the life or an idol like money and what it brings will replace Him. Another facet of pride is covetousness wherein the love of wealth and materialism leads to greed. When one loves these things and points their whole life toward their attainment, the demonic force behind the object is actually what is loved.

The love of money in its use and misuse has caused great hardship and hardening to God's Spirit. There has been more division, war, moral decline, murder, soulish depravity, slavery, and diabolical violence manifested through the love and conquest of money than from any other vice. Jesus said that the love of money is a root of ALL evil. True, there are other roots, but this one is pervasive and certainly can prove to be the strongest.

Money itself is not evil. On the contrary, using money as a servant is useful in broadening the Kingdom. But wealth cannot be enshrined as controller and goal-setter or it will cause much vexation from driving spirits who will literally wear a person out physically to attain it. It will deaden their spirits to Kingdom living and make true, honest relationships impossible as it supplants human love. Should God entrust you with wealth, it is a secondary blessing to your spiritual storehouse in heaven and is to be respected and kept in its place as such.

Trouble with handling money, its misuse through compulsive credit spending or exorbitant and flashy prideful possession of it by an abuser will trip him right into the snare of the devil. Seeing the problem and hearing God call for repentance and deliverance from it must be followed with a radical change taking place in the lifestyle to prevent further entrapment.

As a suggestion for walking in freedom from bondage to the love of money, it is helpful to make up a family budget that is reasonable to provide basic needs and repay all outstanding debts. Then as God leads, give away any overabundance—each week. At first, giving even a tenth of your income may seem an impossible task. But the higher law of love will go beyond this amount as you listen and obey to give more. And your needs will still be met.

As you walk (and then run) in this truth it will become difficult to keep up with God in His blessing on your life. But don't expect money for money. Expect His blessings of true love coming into and out of you by a generous and humble hand.

"..God opposes the proud but gives grace to the humble." Ja 4:6.

"He has scattered those who were proud in the thoughts of their heart. He has brought down rulers from their thrones, and has exalted those who were humble." Luke 1:51-52 (NAS).

"But godliness WITH CONTENTMENT is great gain. For we brought nothing into the world, and we can take nothing out of it. But if we have food and clothing, we will be content with that. PEOPLE WHO WANT TO GET RICH fall into temptation and a trap and into many foolish and harmful desires that plunge men into ruin and destruction. FOR THE LOVE OF MONEY IS A ROOT OF ALL KINDS OF EVIL. Some people, eager for money, have wandered from the faith and pierced themselves with many griefs." 1 Ti 6:6-10.

Jesus said, "Whoever can be trusted with very little can also be trusted with much, and whoever is dishonest with very little will also be dishonest with much. So if you have not been trustworthy in handling worldly wealth, who will trust you with true riches?" Luke 16:10-11.

Lying Is Gossip, Slander, And Verbal Abuse

Gossip, both telling and listening to slander of another's reputation and character, and verbal abuse are serious ways of keeping the believer out of fellowship with God. Gossip comes from people whose hearts are bitter or fearful and who have enough lowered self-respect or lack of the fear of God to hope that their mild or wild exaggerations will put them in a better light with whom they are gossiping.

Interestingly, the Greek word for devil is *DIABOLOS* meaning Slanderer. To slander means "to make false charges or misrepresentations; to defame and damage a reputation". Slander and gossip do not wait for facts, truth, or proof. Satan is known as the False Accuser who stands before God night and day accusing the brethren (Re 12:10).

Slander is willful, usually pre-meditated, and does spiteful harm for another's downfall. Slander is so commonplace that there are public laws protecting individuals and corporations against it. Slander—as verbal abuse—is a stronger, more aggressive sin used for attacking to wound or kill. It can be lethal against family members or when used in dependent relationships (against hostage, prisoner, wife, employee, child, student) where little protection is possible. Satan has used slander induced by the media on a corporate and national level to subvert truth through propaganda and deceit. Whole nations have fallen from the effects of slander right into the end time plans of Satan.

Verbal abuse is a very destructive form of hatred and is a carrier of curses. This sin can be so subtle in the Christian's mouth, that much negative confession and put-down is loosed. Verbal abuse will kill good friendships, marriages, careers, and families. It does so by the disintegration of the spirits of those it is leveled against and is most grievous to children, spouses, and your pastor or spiritual confidant because these relationships are basic to happiness.

Finally, lying is most serious because it validates gossip, slander, and verbal abuse—all lies that may or may not be mixed with some truth. Speaking lies is the devil's native language. Lying is never cute, white, or told "for one's best interests". A lying tongue must be broken in children and not tolerated in adults. Liars are Satan's helpers to spread darkness and keep other's in bondage to untruth.

Keep awake here! The more Christians open themselves to participating actively (talking) or passively (listening) in gossip, slander and lying, the greater territory Satan conquers within them until they cannot recognize what bitter waters are springing from their hearts and mouths. This is how the army of God shoots each other down and keeps the wounded sick.

Counselors: these sins are to be confessed and repented of. After deliverance of these poisoning roots, reconciliation should be encouraged between those involved in telling and/or listening to gossip and slander and the victims of these sins. In the case of verbal abuse, much reconstruction will be in order in family situations for apology and true repentance which does not allow the use and abuse of the tongue against anyone.

"Then there came out a spirit, and stood before the Lord, and said I will go out, and BE A LYING SPIRIT in the mouth of all his prophets. And the Lord said, thou shalt entice him, and thou shalt also prevail: Go out, and do even so...the Lord hath put a lying spirit in the mouth of these thy prophets, and the Lord hath spoken evil against thee." 2 Chr 18:20-22 (KJV).

"You shall not give false testimony against your neighbor." Ex 20:16.

"Thou shalt not raise a false report: put not thine hand with the wicked to be an unrighteous witness." Ex 23:1 (KJV).

"Ye are of your father the devil, and the lusts of your father ye will do. He was a murderer from the beginning, and abode not in the truth because there is not truth in him. When he speaketh a LIE, he speaketh of his own; for he is a LIAR, and the father of it." Jn 8:44 (KJV).

"But now put them all away: anger, wrath, malice, slander, and foul talk FROM YOUR MOUTH." Col 3:8 (RSV).

"But I (Jesus) tell you that men will have to give account on the day of judgment for EVERY CARELESS WORD THEY HAVE SPOKEN. For by your words you will be acquitted, and by your words you will be condemned." Mt 12:36-37.

"Evil words destroy. Godly skill rebuilds." Pr 11:9.

"..the tongue is a small part of the body but makes great boasts..(it) is a fire, a world of evil among the parts of the body. It corrupts the whole person, sets the whole course of his life on fire, and is itself set on fire by hell...With the tongue we praise our Lord and Father, and with it we curse men, who have been made in God's likeness. Out of the same mouth come praise and cursing. My brothers, this should not be..." James 3:5-12.

The Root Of Anger

ANGER is found in the Hebrew as *QATSAPH* or *CHEMA* meaning "to crack off, burst out in rage, fret self, provoke to wrath, vex, be furious; splintered off by rage or strife; foam, indignation, sore, tempest, vain whirlwind, windy; heat, poison from its fever, hot displeasure." Anger in New Testament Greek is *ORGIZO* and *CHOLAO* meaning "to become exasperated, provoked, contrary to a friend, be rebellious, irritable, enraged, choleric."

Anger which is negative in nature is expressed when a person's perceived "rights" are questioned, countered, or imposed upon. Therefore this protection of self or human rights as expressed in aggressive behavior becomes a tool to dominate and retain the lusts of the flesh. In western cultures, aggressive anger as a behavior is lauded and exemplified in business and politics as "being smart" in order to garner worldly success.

Anger directed at people is never born out of love for the other person. Anger hides behind the attacking, dominating, fear-provoking behavior that is a fleshly response used to keep one's self, possessions (even spouse, children, food), concepts, and control of the situation for one's own benefit. Anger used in this way is contrary to the gentle, Holy Spirit of God and has no place whatever in the believer's life.

Some forms anger may take are malice, bitterness, resentment, being argumentative, intolerant, rebellious, using sedition, clamor, loudness to cause fear (especially destructive to small children), physical and verbal abuse, wrath, envy, gossip, revenge, physical violence, judgment by harsh or directed criticism (they think it is constructive but the corrected person is devastated), temper tantrums, harm to self or others and through attacking or threatening body movements.

Anger is revealed as unforgiveness, contempt, impatience, displeasure, contrariness, irritability, sexual frustration, jealousy, stubbornness, blocked mind to the truth, murder, war, rape, swearing, cursing and foul body language; as challenging authority, exaggeration, aggressive-illegal driving habits, meanness (often seen in sports), and fractious or frivolous lawsuits. An angry personality cannot be pleased no matter what is done or said to please them and is unruly, quarrelsome in public to embarrass someone close to them. Young children or teens display screaming fits. Angry adults shout others down.

Anger is also seen in passive ways as depression (anger turned toward self), obesity, pouting, refusal to communicate, cold hard stares to intimidate, or undermine business deals calculated to cripple and topple another. Passive anger generates addictions and self-destructive diseases such as sleeping, exercising or eating disorders.

Anger is often a person's demonic strongman holding other lesser evil entities within. It becomes a coddled demon if it is allowed to take on forms of behavior which are thought to be "my personality traits". Often fear comes in with anger because the person is fearful of losing control when delivered of anger.

How different it is for Christ's followers! Believers in their surrender to God at salvation, have given over all their rights and control of self by acknowledging the Lordship of Jesus Christ in all life's decisions. When we

Christians begin to realize that we own not one thing of this world—that all things are given to us and ultimately taken from us, we will stop struggling to possess and cease becoming angry when they are threatened.

Any calamity can come and remove all possessions from us and most rapidly. ALL OF EVERYTHING belongs to the Lord. In His love and by design, we are allowed responsibility to use things and love people, for a season. After all, we are the servants, stewards, and managers He left behind to multiply the talents. But we were never told we may keep the talents.

Those who have learned to be willing to give up whatever they temporarily have as a possession know that God has promised back many-fold everything freely given to others in the pursuit of His Kingdom. Certainly a reaction of anger against someone who is trying to take what is "ours" leads to fights, murders, stealing, lies, lawsuits or whatever seems necessary to hold on to the possession.

Regarding possessiveness God says, let go and allow Me the pleasure of meeting your needs. Second Corinthians 4:18 expresses the truth that whatever we can see with our eyes will pass away. And what we cannot see, passes into eternity. It is obvious that the importance of living rests with the eternal valuables: the invisibles of the Spirit. Because of this, we can give up anger.

Here is a final word to those of you who live with or around angry people and become the victim. You must seek God for relief from this environment because it will eventually kill love in a relationship and must be dealt with. Tolerating destructive anger in a life partner, child, or in any relationship is being part and party in the anger. We are not to support weaknesses in others but seek to help them out of the bondage they are in and get out of it ourselves. Happily, God can be trusted with your life and their life! Participating in this anger-bond must be confessed as a lack of trust in the Lord. Repent of it. Soundly reject anger out loud and cut the soul-tie to this person.

Counselors: after praying for deliverance from spirits of anger, the counselee should be advised that at their first opportunity (since anger is so often used against others), forgiveness for this behavior should be sought from those offended. That may be hard to do but it is the only way to allow true, loving relationships be established. Pride will be broken in asking for forgiveness and a Renewed Mind will change the behavior to that which is acceptable to God bringing peace and harmony in that life instead of constant upheaval and destruction.

"My dear brothers, take note of this. Everyone should be QUICK TO LISTEN, SLOW TO SPEAK, AND SLOW TO BECOME AN-GRY, FOR MAN'S ANGER DOES NOT BRING ABOUT THE RIGHTEOUS LIFE THAT GOD DESIRES. Therefore, GET RID of the moral filth and the evil that is so prevalent and HUMBLY ac-cept the word planted in you, which can save you." Ja 1:19-20.

"I want men everywhere to lift up holy hands in prayer, WITHOUT ANGER OR DISPUTING." 1 Ti 2:8.

"If any of you has a DISPUTE with another...one brother goes to law against another—and this in front of unbelievers!.. (v7) The very fact that you have lawsuits among you means you have been com-pletely defeated already. Why not rather be wronged? Why not rather be cheated? Instead, you yourselves cheat and do wrong, and you do this to your brothers." 1 Co 6:1-8.

"MAKE EVERY EFFORT TO LIVE IN PEACE WITH ALL MEN and to be holy; without holiness no one will see the Lord. See that no one misses the grace of God and that NO BITTER ROOT GROWS UP to cause trouble and defile many." Heb 12:14-15.

"Blessing crowns the head of the righteous, but violence over-whelms the mouth of the wicked." Pr 10:6.

"But the fruit of the Spirit is love, joy, peace, patience, kindness, goodness, faithfulness, gentleness and self-control..." Gal 5:22.

When thinking about the roots of sin the Bible speaks about, the Lord compares them with the roots of plants. Some strong plants and trees have a taproot that reaches further than any of the other roots, going for life in the forms of water and needed nutrients. We are to put a taproot into the Holy Spirit.

Still other plants have more complex and scattered root systems. For ex-ample, an oak tree does not have a taproot like other trees but it will have a network of large to smaller roots the same length and pattern under-ground as the branches, limbs, and leaves have above ground. This is for balance and efficiency. Likewise, root sins in a life may go deep into the spirit, soul, and body or branch out touching many auxiliary areas that are only externally seen. The next Chapter will demonstrate this principle concerning the attack against the body and how deeply or broadly the roots of sin are taken advantage of by Satan.

CHAPTER 7

The Attack Against
The Human Body

It is exciting to consider the magnificent physical home for the spirit and soul God gave all humans at creation. The complexity and diversity of this marvelous wonder is still not totally understood by science yet we may enjoy our bodies with all its natural defenses, capacity for pleasure, and ability to take us where we wish to go.

What we do understand is that the body is to be used for His will and glory. It is the outward vehicle by which we relate to the physical world. For the Christian, the body is a sacred temple of the living God and must be treated with care, respect, and holiness (Romans 12:1-2).

In the natural order of life cycles and reproduction, God ordained sexual intercourse for practical and recreational purposes. That is clearly seen in the Song of Solomon. He lovingly set these sexual privileges aside for adult men and women to be enjoyed within the context of the Sacrament of Holy Marriage. Sex is not a past time for children as our culture dictates, but a commitment made to God by married adults.

Respecting sexual relations as God intended gives protection from disease and freedom from guilt and brings the blessing of the Lord for prosperity. When the concept of the body is misused or abused, a person is out of his or her chosen place and has been opened up to Satan's advantage. He or she may find out too late that the Lion has been set free to kill and destroy from within the body.

We must have a healthy love (not adoration) for our bodies so as to live long on the earth as free from pain, disease, early death, and suffering as possible: this is blessing. King David gave himself as a servant especially suited to meet God's purposes to his own generation. He continued to struggle with Jehovah until his relationship between spirit, soul, and body was put in proper balance. Because of this kind of discipline in David's early life, God's testimony sustained the Jewish nation at so critical a time.

David blessed later generations through his blood line as a heritage to Jesus Christ (Acts 13:36).

A special concern to Christian parents in a highly permissive society should be to make available from the church or godly home, Christ-centered sex education. It is an absolute necessity to equip our children scripturally to escape the snare and pressures of illicit sex. Virginity before marriage for both sons and daughters is the only Biblical position. Any alteration of this direction can only damage their tender spirits and enslave the sacredness of their bodies.

And you single Christian adults: a total lack of honor and respect for God's revealed will in your bodies will lead you to either a promiscuous sexual lifestyle or multiple monogamous relationships. Both are sexual self-abuse and defile God's temple. Instead, ask the Lord for the supernatural fruit of self-control to grow in your character so your testimony remains clean and pure from the guilt and torment of evil spirits. You need to be unspotted by the world and in right relationship with God to gain meaning from life.

Two questions you might want to answer are these: Is sex outside of marriage important enough to kill for it (as in abortion should a pregnancy occur)? And, is sex outside of marriage important enough to die for it (as in contracting AIDS)?

Let's look at something very popular in the world right now: over-concern for the body and body-fixation. Both are sin and idolatry. This behavior is manifested in pampering the body into unhealth, over-developing it by extreme muscle use, or surgically changing it for vanity's sake. Has God ever demanded that we look 18 years old all of our lives? Then why believe the devil on chasing the elusiveness of youth?

Some believers are shallowly engaged in constant discussion about illnesses, allergies, diets, and exotic diseases. They are robbers who steal time away from others who wish to speak on the things of the Lord. The Bible says to avoid them (Titus 3:9-11).

Then there is the other group who are convinced that hating their bodies as evil, denying it nutrition, cleanliness, medical attention, proper rest, and exercise is "spiritually prudent". This old tactic of the devil to focus all a believer's attention on the physical was most successful during the Middle Ages but proved fruitless and ungodly, gendering false doctrines that have plagued the Church for centuries. How subtle and diversionary Satan can be!

But when the body is used naturally as a servant and gift from God in balanced perspective, all your much needed time and attention can be devoted to being used as a channel for the Holy Spirit without the encumberance of centering on the physical plane. There is a time for fasting. There is also a time for feasting. Those led by the Spirit of God know when to do both.

Listed are some areas of attack against the body which have been given particular attention here, but there can be many more. Remember, the mind is the battleground: it is in the mind that choices are made to sin or not to sin, to walk with the Lord, or to walk after the fleshly appetites.

Sexual Immorality, Perversion, Bestiality

1. ADULTERY is sexual sin when at least one of the partners is married: is in violation of the marriage vow; it corrupts or makes poorer by mixing with an inferior strength. Sexual union is spiritual union and reserved for marriage only (1 Cor 7). The marriage covenant is a three-way promise between God and man, God and woman, man and woman. Adultery breaks this covenant by introducing alien affection through the decision to sin.

God's way is to keep the marriage covenant pure. As an example, the Church is a type of the spotless Bride presented to God's Son in spiritual marriage. Thus a Godly marriage produces the fruit of love, children, pleasure and fun, mental and emotional stability, longer life, a partnership to stand against the powers of the world and Satan, companionship and comfort in old age.

Love in a marriage is an attitude of the mind, not a weak sentimental emotion that is easily diverted by someone new. Lust is demonic and there is no love in it. Love is Godly (1 Pe 3:1-7). The Lord continually declares that He hates adultery; in fact, He divorced His wife Israel for the spiritual whoredoms she committed with the world and His archenemy, Satan, by her idolatrous living.

First Corinthians 6:15-20 deals with a person (male or female) who is not in God's order. The physical body is spoken of as members (part) of Christ Himself. Even today, almost two thousand years later after this was written, Paul asks the pointed question to someone contemplating adultery, *"Shall I then take the members of Christ and unite them with a prostitute? Never! Do you not know that he who unites himself with a prostitute is one with her in body? For it is said, 'The two will become one flesh'. But he who unites himself with God is one with him in spirit."* It is an abomination to submit Christ within you (who goes everywhere with you) to an illicit and filthy sexual experience. How that grieves the Holy Spirit and damages the human spirit.

Temptation to commit adultery must be rejected outright. If you are in a situation or work place where you are constantly tempted to sin, the believer MUST make direct assault against the demon and make his or her position known to the tempter. Regard it as a direct and evil assault against your marital commitment and desire for godliness. Don't allow Satan to flatter your vanity by flirting with sexual temptation. You will lose. Do not even give the appearance of evil by placing yourself in situations with people that can be construed as wrong. Take responsibility for your marriage vows and for keeping the door shut in Satan's face.

Some tormenting demons that can come in with adultery are rebellion, lust, liar, covenant breaker, perversion, pride, unfaithfulness, anger, prostitution, jezebel or ahab spirit, selfishness, idolater, crime, regret, guilt, self-hate, spouse-hate, rejection, and jealousy.

"FLEE (don't walk but run) FROM SEXUAL IMMORALITY. ALL other sins a man commits are outside his body, but he who sins sexually sins against his own body. Do you not know that YOUR BODY IS THE TEMPLE OF THE HOLY SPIRIT WHO IS IN YOU, whom you have received from God? You are not your own; you were bought at a price. Therefore honor God with your body." 1 Co 6:18-20.

"THOU shalt not commit adultery." Ex 20:14 (KJV).

"You have heard that it was said by them of old time, Thou shalt not commit adultery: But I say to you that whosoever looketh on a woman to lust after her hath committed adultery with her already in his heart. And if thy right eye offend thee, pluck it out, and cast it from thee; for it is profitable for thee that one of thy members should perish, and not that thy whole body should be cast into hell." Mt 5:27-29 (KJV).

"But whoso committeth adultery with a woman lacketh understanding: HE THAT DOETH IT DESTROYETH HIS OWN SOUL. A wound and dishonor shall he get; and his reproach shall not be wiped away." Pr 6:32-35 (KJV).

2. FORNICATION is all sexual impurity between two (or more) unmarried. The Hebrew words for fornication are *TAZNUTH* and *ZANAH* meaning, "harlotry, idolatry, fornication; cause to be, to play, to

fall to whoredom, to go a-whoring continually". The New Testament GREEK word is *PORNEUO* or, "to act the harlot, indulge unlawful lust (of either sex), practice idolatry, commit fornication."

I can find no place in Scripture where a pure, holy sexual relationship does or can exist between people who are not joined in marriage. It is explicitly given for Christians NOT to engage in premarital sex of any kind. Just look at what Paul said in 1 Corinthians 5:9-11, "..I wrote to you in an epistle not to company with fornicators". The Lord is concerned not only with our indulging in this sin personally, but also places a high standard against forming and maintaining friendships with those practicing fornication.

"For this is the will of God, EVEN YOUR SANCTIFICATION that ye should ABSTAIN FROM FORNICATION." 1 Th 4:3 (KJV).

"Let not sin therefore reign in your mortal body, that ye should obey it in the lusts thereof. Neither yield ye your members as instruments of unrighteousness unto sin: but yield yourselves unto God, as those that are alive from the dead, and your MEMBERS AS INSTRUMENTS OF RIGHTEOUSNESS unto God." Ro 6:12-13 (KJV).

"Put to death, therefore, whatever belongs to your earthly nature: SEXUAL IMMORALITY, IMPURITY, LUST, EVIL DESIRES AND GREED, which is idolatry." Col 3:5.

"Those controlled by the sinful nature CANNOT PLEASE God." Ro 8:8.

3. INCEST means to have willful sexual relations with a relative (Greek word is *PORNEIA*) by blood or close lawful kinships.

"No one is to approach ANY CLOSE RELATIVE to have sexual relations. I am the Lord." Lev 18:6.

"Thus were both the daughters of Lot with child by their father." Ge 19:36 (KJV).

The consequences of these incestuous relationships resulted in a severe penalty to the offspring as seen in Deuteronomy 23:2-3: "A bastard shall not enter into the congregation of the Lord; even to his tenth generation shall he not enter into the congregation of the Lord. An Ammonite or a Moabite shall not enter into the congregation of the Lord." The wicked tribes of Ammon and Moab were the result of incest between Lot and his two daughters.

"If a man sleeps with his father's wife, he has dishonored his father. Both the man and the woman must be put to death; their blood will be on their own heads. If a man sleeps with his daughter-in-law, both of them must be put to death. What they have done is a perversion..if a man marries both a woman and her mother, it is wicked...If a man marries his sister, the daughter of either his father or his mother, and they have sexual relations it is a disgrace. They must be cut off...Do not have sexual relations with a sister..for it would dishonor a close relative. If a man sleeps with his aunt, he dishonores his uncle. If a man marries his brother's wife, it is an act of impurity..." Le 20:11-21.

"You are to deliver this man over to Satan for physical discipline to destroy carnal lusts (which prompted him to incest) that (his) spirit may (yet) be saved in the day of the Lord Jesus." 1 Co 5:5 (AMP).

4. BESTIALITY is performing sexually with animals and is an abomination and loathful thing before the Lord. Besides sinning against your own body, it debases the honor and position God has given the human being above animals and other creation. The AIDS virus and some venereal diseases are said to have passed into the human system as a result of participating in sex with animals.

It has been increasingly difficult to find cures for sexually transmitted diseases when different strains are mixed together from multiple partners. This perverted sex is cursed of the Lord. God's way is to abstain from all sex or be committed to a life-long marriage (male with female) in faithfulness.

"Cursed is the man who has sexual relations with any animal." De 27:21.

"Neither shalt thou lie with any beast to defile thyself therewith: neither shall any woman stand before a beast to lie down thereto: it is confusion." Le 18:23 (KJV).

"If a man has sexual relations with an animal, he must be put to death and you must kill the animal. If a woman approaches an animal to have sexual relations with it, kill both." Lev 20:15-16.

5. HOMOSEXUAL, LESBIAN, BISEXUAL SIN. The Old Testament Hebrew for this sin is *QADESH* or, "a (male) devotee (by prostitution) to licentious idolatry; a sodomite, unclean." From the Greek word *PORNOS*, we get this definition: "a (male) prostitute, a debauchee (libertine); fornicator, whoremonger."

All homosexual activity must be confessed as rebellion in order to become free of it. It is possible for a male or female to have this demon though never practiced, and is often one of the causes that destroys normal male-female ways of relating. These unclean spirits come through sexual relations with people who have practiced perverted sex with others and may be passed through ancestry.

Many demons are introduced into the person of the rebellious and practicing sodomite. The Bible refers to those who practice sexual intimacy with members of their same sex as "sodomites". Genesis 19 reveals the awesome and total destruction God visited on the towns of Sodom and Gomorrah because of the prevailing cities-wide practice of homosexuality. These sites remain uninhabited. The Bible calls these people sodomites, not gays, lesbians, queers or other demeaning labels that serve to mask the seriousness of this sin.

Clergymen who are in bondage to this sin and are nevertheless ordained to the ministry by "understanding" spiritual authorities are in special danger. First, they have been betrayed by people who should know the Word of God more perfectly (2 Tim 4:3), and second, they are encouraged to continue (and sometimes defiantly) to be enslaved and lead others under their care into sin by example (James 3:1).

Auxiliary spirits that may enter are hate, lust, fear of sex, lack of identity, perversion (mental and physical), pornography, sadism, unclean spirits (anal sex), child molestation, rape, vulgarity, voyeurism (peeping tom), indecency (lack of modesty), torture, confusion, cowardice, fetishes, spirit of darkness, spiritual blindness, strip-tease, dirty dancing, attention spirit, tatoo-scarification, defiance, promiscuity, idol of physical pleasures, flashing and mooning (desire to expose genitals), transvestite, sensuality, luring and inticing spirits, militancy, and anger. You can see that this is a large doorway to torment.

"Thou shalt not lie with mankind, as with womankind: It is an abomination." Le 18:22 (KJV).

"The woman shall not wear that which pertaineth unto a man, neither shall a man put on a woman's garment: for all that do so, are abomination unto the Lord thy God." De 22:5 (KJV).

"There shall be no whore of the daughters of Israel, nor a sodomite of the sons of Israel." De 23:17 (KJV).

"Therefore God gave them over in the sinful desires of their hearts to SEXUAL IMPURITY for the degrading of their bodies with one another. They exchanged the truth of God for a lie, and worshiped and served created things rather than the Creator, who is forever praised. Amen. Because of this, God gave them over to shameful lusts. Even their women exchanged natural relations for unnatural ones. In the same way the men also ABANDONED NATURAL RELATIONS with women and were inflamed with lust for one another. Men committed indecent acts with other men, and received IN THEMSELVES THE DUE PENALTY for their PERVERSION." Ro 1:24-32.

"In a similar way, Sodom and Gomorrah and the surrounding towns GAVE THEMSELVES UP TO SEXUAL IMMORALITY AND PERVERSION. They serve as an example of those who suffer the punishment of eternal fire. In the same way, these dreamers POLLUTE THEIR OWN BODIES, reject authority and slander celestial beings...Yet these men speak abusively against whatever they do not understand; and what things they do understand by instinct, like unreasoning animals—these are the very things that destroy them." Jude 7,9.

Rejection: The Two-Edged Sword

What happens to those of us who have experienced rejection as a natural consequence of being a living human, yet have failed to overcome this negativism and thereby have moved into mental and emotional unhealth? Are there answers in deliverance from being the victims as well as the perpertrators of rejection?

Primarily, the feelings of rejection arise from a life-long pattern often beginning in childhood and reinforced throughout life. It gives terrible guilt to not measuring up, or being different from the group therefore unwanted, or failing in some way to meet "acceptable" standards of behavior.

The bad effects of rejection are felt by those not walking in the protection of the blood of Jesus through either their own warfare, or as a child not sheltered by the guidance, loving support, and believing prayer of a significant person(s) during those childhood years. This lack of cover opens a gap in the personality to the demon of rejection, causing them to continue to behave "rejected" as a lifestyle pattern, serving to reinforce the demon influence. People who are engulfed by rejection perceive rejection by others even when it is not the case.

The root of rejection comes from a self-centeredness that is made worse by a constant suspicious vigilance against allowing others to come close emotionally in case they go away which results in more rejection or the fear of failure. Fear of man, unbelief, and loss of confidence are cohabiting demons, strengthening rejection's vicious grasp.

The key to gaining freedom over rejection is in FORGIVENESS of yourself, forgiveness to all those who have hurt you, as well as forgiveness of God Himself. This last surprising source is possible if you are angry with Him over your experiences of suffering from either feeling or being rejected.

The Effects of Rejection

People who suffer from the effects of rejection can have some or many of these twenty characteristics:

1. Is emotionally immature from short-stopping relationship development; patterns of divorce, constant move, and change.
2. Displays a self-centeredness (Bob Mumford's black-hole theory) expressed by constant requests of: "pray for me, help me, love me, see me, teach me, listen to me, feed me…".
3. Has an unstable back-and-forth Christian walk.
4. Shows a lack of commitment to the Christian walk, to the family, to a hobby, to someone special, a spouse, friends, to a Bible group, earning a living, or just "being there" when needed by another.
5. Obvious low self-identity, feelings of inferiority with a need to question God's love and care for them.
6. Suffers from loneliness (even at a gathering) and continually builds walls through their language, actions, or gestures to keep people distant.
7. May have grown up under perfectionism and "earned" approval by their actions, grades, athletic skills, or outward appearance.
8. Is a people-pleaser without strong feelings that would counter some

one important in life (this is passive side).

9. Feels betrayed easily and is offended at even casual snubs.

10. Worries, has doubts and fears of failure, shows anxiety and unbelief for success and may actually bring financial insecurity on self to reinforce the rejection cycle.

11. Has allowed a physical handicap to dominate all of life.

12. May have been over-protected (smothered) as a child or as a change-of-life baby, as adopted; by being a child of the "wrong sex", or by coming from a broken home, having the mother die at your birth, or being a mixed race baby. It is easy to seek people or places to blame or justify feelings of rejection.

13. Feels (or is) unloved for just being "me".

14. Is often suspicious and may feel persecuted.

15. Acts impatient and intolerant of slow movers, slow thinkers, inept drivers, the infirm or anyone else who does not share their world view.

16. May develop stress diseases (i.e., high blood pressure) or takes it out on physical body by finding comfort in over-eating, drinking, smoking, drugs, and depression.

17. Is quick tempered, argumentative, angry, clashes easily with people closest to them (passive types withdraw at conflict).

18. Must constantly receive credit, adoration, stroking, and personal validation by anyone.

19. Has trouble submitting—will quit first—rather than work with others; drives to lead or withdraws totally.

20. Is critical and a moralist; knows how to fix everything and "put it back into order".

The Six Postures of Rejection

The following soul-positions that rejected people take help them deal in their own strength with the stresses of life. This in not an exhaustive study, but serves to help uncover the camouflage that rejection puts into a personality to keep one from open and transparent living. Working from a posture whose core is soulish deters the human spirit from rightful headship and lacks that constant checking in with the Holy Spirit for correct personality allignment and development.

1. THE BRAGGART. Exaggerates even small accomplishments (golf scores, fish lengths, sales, amount of money in pocket, child's feats). Stories are told to get recognition, to become "bigger than life", to get self-worth. It is upheld by lying spirits, unfaithfulness, fear, and intimidation.

2. CRITICAL. Easily adapts to his or her own situation because it is narrowly defined by their own concept of right and wrong; they are quick to point out other's faults (especially in areas they feel accomplished). A critical spirit is actually pride ("I'm not where you are, poor dear") and promotes spiritual blindness, lack of love, and intolerance.

3. THE LONER. Has a wounded spirit (from real or imagined hurts) and forms walls of protection all around. This is actually a lack of faith in God to BE and DO ALL that she or he feels are needs. It fortifies unbelief, pain, loneliness, emotional atrophy, creating a "little child" spirit which will hinder maturing.

4. DEFIANT and REBELLIOUS. Bucks the system; may become very aggressive or bullying to prove one's self worthy to authorities or in his or her own household. It often shows itself as a workaholic and over-achiever to gain materialistically or goes all out for fame and public recognition which is believed to be a strong extension of themselves. Collaborating spirits are a deceptive spirit, rebellion, mean and abusive spirits, murder, pride, competitive spirit, criminal and negativity.

5. SHY and RETIRING. This posture is very insidious and manipulative. Shyness is a controlling spirit masked in timidity, bashfulness, and wariness. It is used in hope of changing the behavior of a child, parent, spouse, friend, co-worker or group to do things to his or her own advantage. It manifests itself in a lack of courage to make decisions openly and reflects inward anger. Sickness, self-pity and controller are sometimes allowed to cohabit by the spirit of rejection.

Acting shy is an excuse and ploy to avoid being mature in demanding situations. Shyness should be prayed and trained out of children. It is interesting to realize that Jesus was meek, never shy. Meekness is humility, a strength of character.

6. SWITCH-HITTING. This is the hypocritical mask of rejection where, even though he or she is highly critical of others, cannot stand criticism directed toward themselves and are above being questioned. Or, if one behavior is expected of them, they will change to please even though they previously stood against it.

Taking a switch-hitting posture comes out of a lack of strong identity in

Christ and the responsibility to take the good with the bad when motives, actions, opinions, or personal beliefs are questioned. Mature people will either stand by their decisions as correct or apologize for error when proven wrong but will not deny the action taken. Allied spirits are liar, double-minded, indecisive, smokescreen and hypocrite.

Our Father desires us to have very strong beliefs and ideas of who we are. We get these healthy postures from simply evaluating ourselves and where we are regarding our character then looking intently at the Word of God to see our spiritual and (many times) physical and soul positions in Christ.

The Holy Spirit makes this possible through the gentle proddings of our consciences that point out sin or a wrong path taken. Godly character is formed when the Holy Spirit is obeyed and we consistently turn in God's direction. A person who knows they have heard from and have been obedient to the Lord will not allow the feelings of rejection to enter because of the misguided opinions all around. Security comes in knowing you are in God's will. That is when you know who you are. Expect to be different but all right.

Making It Work In Deliverance

Rejection is a two-edged sword because the one suffering from being rejected often turns around and rejects others from a self-defense stance. Both the reaction (being rejected) and the action (rejecting others) must be dealt with.

Now is the time to get free by confessing out loud your forgiveness even if some of those who have rejected you or whom you have rejected, are now dead (like parents, an old employer or teacher, ex-spouse). Just go ahead and forgive them from your heart as a decision of your will. You will find this to be very cleansing to the innerman that will loose all those tight bands that have held you back from experiencing life with joy. This takes work on your part but remember, this is YOUR deliverance and you have determined to be set free.

It might help to first look at all the following verses God gave for you to know how unique you are. You are special! And if everybody DID walk away, you would still be in the majority standing with your Lord alone. He understands.

"Know that the Lord is God. It is He who made us, and WE ARE HIS PEOPLE, THE SHEEP OF HIS PASTURE." Ps 100:3.

Chapter 7

"And God saw EVERYTHING that He made, and behold, IT WAS VERY GOOD." Ge 1:31 (KJV).

"This is what the Lord says, your Redeemer, who FORMED YOU IN THE WOMB; I am the Lord, who has made all things." Is 44:24; 43:7; 49:1,5 and Jer 1:5).

"You made all the delicate, inner parts of my body, and knit them together in my mother's womb. Thank you for making me so wonderfully complex! It is amazing to think about. Your workmanship is marvelous - and how well I know it!" Ps 139:13-14 (LIV).

"For though my father and my mother forsake me, the Lord will take care of me." Ps 27:10 (BERK).

"..wherein HE HATH MADE US ACCEPTED IN THE BELOVED." Ep 1:6 (KJV).

"He (Jesus Christ) is DESPISED and REJECTED of men; a man of sorrows, and acquainted with grief: and we hid as it were our faces from him, he was despised, and we esteemed him not." (NOTE: Because Christ was rejected, He understands us and nailed that to the cross along with all sin and suffering.) Is 53:3 (KJV).

"The Spirit of the Lord is upon me (Jesus), because He hath anointed me to preach the gospel to the poor; He hath sent me TO HEAL THE BROKENHEARTED, TO PREACH DELIVERANCE TO THE CAPTIVES, and the recovering of sight to the blind, TO SET AT LIBERTY THEM THAT ARE BRUISED." Lk 4:18 (KJV) and Is 61:1.

"For I will restore health unto thee, and I will heal thee of thy wounds, saith the Lord; because THEY CALLED THEE AN OUTCAST, saying, This is Zion, whom no man seeketh after". Jer 30:17(KJV). (NOTE: God promised healing for all the wounds that have come out of rejection and will deliver from all allied spirits which entered by that wound.)

"But the Lord said unto Samuel, 'LOOK NOT ON HIS COUNTENANCE, OR ON THE HEIGHT OF HIS STATURE; because

I have refused him; for the LORD SEETH NOT AS MAN SEETH: FOR A MAN LOOKETH ON THE OUTWARD APPEARANCE, BUT THE LORD LOOKETH ON THE HEART.' " 1 Sa 16:7 (KJV).

"And the Lord said unto him, 'Who hath made man's mouth? or who maketh the dumb, or deaf, or the seeing, or the blind? have not I, the Lord?' " Ex 4:11 (KJV).

Because our inner being is supremely important to God, any physical disabilities we may have are invisible to Him. God cannot reject His own creation but loves to take each of us just as we are. Even extreme beauty or handsomeness as the world defines it can disable many from seeking a closeness with God through false pride. Believe God that you are physically acceptable. Thank Him for your body and praise Him that He has allowed you to live and serve Him in very unique ways!

Counselors: take time and care with this area of having the counselees forgive everyone by name (first name only is sufficient) because it is integral to completing the basics toward full liberation. In one person we worked with, it took the better part of three hours to get through forgiveness alone because the hurts were so deep. But how quickly the time went in actual deliverance after these roots were gently dug up by the hand of the counselee that was guided by the Holy Spirit!

Depression—The Black Hole

The ancient way depression is described uses two Hebrew words. *'EBAL* describes a mourning, lamenting, moaning; to bewail, chant and wail. This is the acute stage of mourning coming after a calamity and is a natural and healthy expression of great loss. *BALAH,* however, brings with it the results of carrying mourning too far or falling into a depression. It means to "fail, decay, consume, spend, waste; to make dusty and black as sackcloth, sordid garments."

Deuteronomy 26:14 uses the Hebrew word *'AVEN* to show that the man who came to offer his sacred portion (a tenth of the firstfruits for the priests, widows, and orphans) did not do so when he was in a period of mourning. That type of mourning of the spirit (depression) was not a blessed attitude with which to offer to the Lord his sacred portion. God truly means He loves a cheerful giver with healthy motivations behind the gift.

'AVEN however, means "to pant (hence exert oneself in vain; to come to naught); strickly nothingness. Also trouble, vanity, wickedness, an idol: affliction, evil, false idol, iniquity, mischief, mourners and mourning, naught, sorrow, unjust, unrighteous, vain, vanity, wickedness and idolatry". Again, God was very careful that His peoples' attitudes were right as they gave themselves to spiritual service.

From Job 3:8, mourning is translated by the Hebrew as LIVYATHAN or, "a wreathed animal, a serpent; the constellation of the dragon; a symbol of Babylonia: leviathan, mourning." Dragons as symbols for Satan and Babylon, represented the world system in opposition to God's kingdom throughout the ages. Look how closely depression is intertwined with these two sources. In practice, Leviathan may have had more than one head. Ask the Holy Spirit to reveal how many heads are on the Leviathan and then ask their names. Cut these exposed heads off by the Holy Spirit then cast out the beast and all his heads in deliverance.

While researching Livyathan, I found the subsidiary word LAVAH having to do with "borrowing, to unite; to borrow as a form of obligation or to lend: abide with the borrower, to cleave and join oneself with a lender" (this creates an unholy soul-tie). This may help explain how destructive and depressive credit borrowing has been for many Christians who must find enough money to pay debts while food, proper shelter, and funds for the Lord take a subservient place. This is real bondage.

Let's look at Ezekiel 2:10 where depression is spoken of as HEGEH, "a muttering, sighing, thought, sound of thunder; murmuring (in pleasure or anger), sore imaginations." This subtle form of depression attacks the soul in the intellect and emotions with consequences manifested outwardly.

As we go into the New Testament meanings in the Greek, DUO enlarges our understanding to include, "to sink, go down, set", while ODUREMOS brings out the aspect of "mourning, to lament, sorrow and torment (Mt 2:18)". From James 4:9 and Rev 18:8, come PATHO and ENTHOS, "to grieve, mourn and sorrow; to experience a sensation or impression (usually painful); feel, have passion, suffer, vex."

Depression is a very serious condition that Satan can create from without. But he cannot do it without the Christian's consent. It is allowed to station itself within by embracing an unbelief in God to move on your behalf in some particular situation that is "depressing". Unfortunately, we can become our own worse enemies by using fleshly interior motives to bring it upon ourselves. That is the embracing aspect of depression.

The good news is that by God's loving grace, we can also be rid of it in the name of Jesus Christ by resisting it through the renewing of our mind.

It takes work.

Depression is anger turned inward. It is an internal temper tantrum that is damaging to the whole person. Medical science has found specific chemical responses in the brains of depressed persons unlike chemicals of the non-depressed. This leaves us with the question: is depression caused by brain-manufactured chemicals or are brain-manufactured chemicals caused by the negative human response to the upsetting or unpleasant occurances in life? What responses do we make in our spirits that can produce physical change?

Depressive spirits are usually strongly linked with the "strongman" (chief demon or head of the demon family). For example, Hatred can be a strongman which gains entry through the act of child abuse bringing about unresolved guilt and finally, depression spirits with it. When Depression itself is the strongman, it will make room for, say, a suicide spirit because these feed on each other. Families of demons link themselves together for reinforcement and mutual feeding.

Fighting against what God brings into your life out of fear or rebellion at a possible negative result, is a secondary type of depression. It comes from feeling inadequate for what one views as a hardship instead of bringing the positive faith-attitude of experiencing a wonderful (if not, difficult), opportunity to know God more fully.

We are told in James 1:2-4 to *"..consider it PURE JOY (not pure depression!) my brothers, whenever you face trials of many kinds, because you know that the testing of your faith develops perseverance. Perseverance (sticking to something tough until you get through) must finish its work so that you may be mature and complete, not lacking anything."* Here we see that the heart-attitude is to be one of cheerful abandon when trials come, not to get down under the circumstances and grovel there.

It is imperative that the spirit of depression not find a home in a Christian. It is possible to be delivered of spirits of depression or never to contract them when a constant guard is mounted against entry or re-entry. The nature of this demon gains strength when the same rebellious, lack of faith reaction to circumstances becomes a behavior pattern. Then it is much more difficult to break. It is preferable, although sometimes most trying, to push beyond depression into maturity. These are the phases of every believer's spiritual growth.

I believe the Lord wants all His children to go into maturity and He will make a way for them to do that: again, TRUST HIM. When a great change for you comes along like divorce, death in the family, the loss of job or business, a new baby in the house, or anything potentially depressing, you can begin right there to praise God for another step to being conformed to the mind of Christ. The victory is in your attitude and the battle is fought in the spirit.

DO NOT GIVE IN TO FEAR OR DEPRESSION. PRAISE AND BELIEVE GOD. STAY IN THE WORD AND CLOSE TO LOVING, BELIEVING FRIENDS FOR SUPPORT THROUGH THESE TIMES. REFUSE, REJECT, AND FIGHT OFF DEPRESSION!

Also, keep busy with living. Discipline yourself to do the little hateful jobs you've been putting off. You will find that working through difficult times with praise in your heart is an act of faith. Get in the Word of God. Life can only be lived from one moment to the next, not years in advance. Depression cannot occupy where faith resides—there is not enough room!

The Human Tripartite And Depression

Depression is found in the human tripartite and may enter in any one or all its areas by the consent of the person. Let us now look at how and why it enters each area.

1. The Human Spirit. This is the part within us that communicates in the spiritual realms. It is the core that cries out to worship God when everything else is not enough to satisfy the God-longing each human experiences. Unsaved people communicate with Satan in their spirits (the worship of pagan idols, occultic activity, sects), but are shut off from God until Jesus Christ is acknowledged as Savior and Lord (Mt 11:27; John 8:42-47). Its place is one of headship over the soul and body in obeying God.

Depression enters as a result of willful sin and disobedience to God. The consequences of the sin (guilt, curse, disaster, vexation) causes a mourning in the spirit (see Ezekiel 7:14-27) that is healthy if it leads to repentance and reconciliation with the Lord. However, if repentance is not attained, a person will mourn to the point of groveling in the guilt, curse, disaster, and vexation until depression is brought on. Depression allowed to come to full bloom will lead to thoughts of suicide. If acted on, these result in death.

What a road downhill! Instead of taking that devilish path, doesn't it make spiritual sense to humble one's self, ask God's forgiveness, turn from the sin and depression, learn from the experience, and then forget it as God forgets it? It will take time to walk through that process but health is guaranteed.

Realize that we WILL fail many times because we are created to be ever-learning. God made provision for our lapses (present and future) and learning snags. Otherwise we would never need Christ Jesus except for a salvation ticket to glory. No! He provided us with continual cleansing and future cycles of growth that build on what we have learned THROUGH OUR MISTAKES.

It does great harm in the spirit to be angry and rebellious until you are sick, putting your ministry on the shelf. Satan loves that sort of victory where believers are not as powerful for God as they are equipped to be and are certainly not keeping him on the run where he belongs.

2. The Human Soul. This is the part of us the world calls "the psychological" but what Christians know as that which relates most naturally with and to other humans. It is the seat of the will, emotions, feelings, mind and intellect. Personality is seen and expressed out of the soul. Its place is one of submission to the spirit.

Allowance for depression may be tolerated in times when expectations are not met or when "the deal fell through". It can happen if your child fails a grade, your spouse breaks faithfulness, your priest/pastor did not validate you *as you thought he should.* For some, depression comes in when you or a family member are jailed, the car blows up, your credit is ruined, your girl- or boyfriend says you are ugly, someone is suing you, or your nation loses the war. We could mention any number of excuses to become depressed. Literally, any mishap dealing with the intellect, will, or emotions is a soft spot Satan first looks for to tempt with depression.

If the believer reacts with anger at the trial instead of counting it all joy, he or she will became (by choice) depressed. Following this decision, self-pity (the emotions of anger, worthlessness, and self-hatred) is invited to abide with depression (it is more comfortable to "feel" sorry for yourself when depressed). Again, this cycle must be cut off before it develops.

A danger area to the soul is to submit it to world-inspired psychological or intellectual persuits in trying to understand one's self or others to handle life's problems. Both are dead ends leading to futile depression. The soul, left in charge, is attracted to closed-circuited methods the world offers (Satan's kingdom) for finding answers to actual spiritual problems. Worldly wisdom is untruth as God presents it and demands an internal scrutinizing of the self which certainly holds no answers.

3. The Human Body. The physical body is the "outer man" and was created to be a source of delight, utility, and practicality for the housing of our inner soul and spirit. It contains the senses of sight, smell, touch, taste, and hearing. It relates us to the physical world of wind, water, fire, vegetable and animal life. Its place is one of submission to the spirit.

This physical area reveals the spritual attack of depression by manifesting itself in the body. It may be seen as obesity, bulemia, addictive disorders, drug-related sicknesses, uncontrolled mourning, and hysterics. It shows up as a lack of interest in life affecting work habits and disrupts marriages and relationships with Father.

Depression can be induced and will be encouraged by the person who abuses the body through overwork, underwork and boredom, improper or multiple fad diets, lack of rest, severe confinement of space or lack of privacy, giving in to peer pressure that goes against better judgment (innerman), and the like. You know what you allow to depress you.

Medication will not stop this behavioral response to difficulties but serves to mask them, making one far too weak to fight and resist in the spirit. Consequently, yet another host of masking demons will be allowed in from relying on chemical and psychological means. It only serves to strengthen the depression cycle. The folly here is the refusal to rely on God in trial. BE CAREFUL.

DEPRESSION MUST BE RENOUNCED AS REBELLION, WITCHCRAFT, IDOLATRY, AND UNBELIEF. DO NOT ALLOW IT TO DAMAGE YOUR PHYSICAL BODY.

I want to encourage you a bit more here to go the distance. Ask the Lord to open your eyes and ears by becoming aware—instantly—to any depressive spirit that wishes to gain entrance. When you hear or feel your spirit begin to sag, fight it right where it raises its head. Tell it:

"NO, YOU FOUL DEPRESSION DEMON, YOU CANNOT FIND A HOME IN ME. GOD IS MY STRENGTH AND SHIELD, A PRESENT HELP IN THIS TIME OF TROUBLE. I CHOOSE JOY, NOT DEATH, RIGHT NOW IN THE NAME OF JESUS CHRIST."

Be vigilant. Be persistant. You will overcome. Here are some precious verses to see God's view of depression and to help build your spirit:

"O Lord, do not rebuke me in your anger or discipline me in your wrath. For your arrows have pierced me, and your hand has come down upon me. Because of your wrath there is no health in my body; my bones have no soundness BECAUSE OF MY SIN. MY GUILT HAS OVERWHELMED ME LIKE A BURDEN TOO HEAVY TO BEAR. My wounds fester and are loathsome because of my sinful folly. I AM BOWED DOWN AND BROUGHT VERY LOW: ALL DAY LONG I GO ABOUT MOURNING.

"My back is filled with searing pain; there is no health in my body. I am FEEBLE AND UTTERLY CRUSHED; I GROAN IN AN-GUISH OF HEART. All my longings lie open before you, O Lord; my sighing is not hidden from you. My heart pounds, my strength fails me; even the light has gone from my eyes." Ps 38:1-10. NOTE: this is a result of sin in the spirit spilled over into the body which also suffers.

"The Lord works righteousness and justice FOR ALL THE OP-PRESSED..The Lord is compassionate and gracious, slow to anger, abounding in love. He will not always accuse, nor will he harbor his anger forever; he does not treat us AS OUR SINS DESERVE or re-pay us according to our iniquities. FOR AS HIGH AS THE HEAVENS ARE ABOVE THE EARTH, SO GREAT IS HIS LOVE FOR THOSE WHO FEAR HIM." Ps 103:6-11.

"You turned my ailing into dancing: you removed my sackcloth and clothed me with joy." Ps 30:11.

"To appoint unto them that mourn in Zion, to give unto them BEAUTY FOR ASHES, the OIL OF JOY FOR MOURNING, the GARMENT OF PRAISE FOR THE SPIRIT OF HEAVINESS; that they might be called trees of righteousness, the planting of the Lord, that he might be glorified." Isa 61:3 (KJV).

"The Spirit of the Lord is upon me...he hath sent me TO HEAL THE BROKEN HEARTED..." Lk 4:18 (KJV).

Chapter 7

Suicide Of The Human Tripartite

All suicide is the willful, premeditated act of taking one's own life. Suicide can occur in the mind (soul), in the spirit, and in the body. It is sin because it is the ultimate rebellion and cannot be repented of. People who wish for and act on suicide impulses say in effect, "I WILL (to) take my life WHEN and HOW I CHOOSE and not how and when God chooses to end His service of my life."

Suicide is cowardly and comes from a distorted or ignorant understanding of God's nature Who is LOVE. People who play with suicide take pleasure in using the threat of it as a manipulation of others for their own benefit. Threatening (and carrying out) suicide is an immature response to crises and should not be tolerated by yourself or by anyone in your home.

Counselors must always remain uncritical and open to those who wish to express their deep response to hurt and the thoughts of suicide. It should be made very plain that suicide is not a consideration for a Christian. God has given other alternatives to solving the most difficult of problems. Agree with the counselee that facing the consequences of resolving problems can be very painful, but God is here to tell you that suicide is not an option. What a relief to believe that by His grace they can grow through this dark valley and not shortcut His methods through open rebellion and anger.

Help for those trapped by suicidal spirits is found by the faithful application of His Word, through Christian counseling, by remaining open to relatives and friends who love and care, and by the Body of Christ who can offer relief through deliverance.

1. Spiritual Suicide occurs when the believer chooses a lie over the Truth of God; gets into the Occult, sets up false idols in the soul, supplants the Word of God by false teaching thereby leading others into false doctrine (even "innocently"); by rejecting the gifts and callings of God; by determined and prolonged grieving of the Holy Spirit to move and act in you; by rejecting the formation of the Mind of Christ within.

2. Suicide of the Soul occurs when a Christian prostitutes God-given mores and values for unseemly gain; decreases mental alertness and responsibilities through vain philosophies to pleasure the intellect; by living a worldly lifestyle that coverts with the devil through acting from totally emotional responses; through coveting the benefits of materialism, money, illicit sex, possessions, power and fame; by habitually acting on its own behalf.

3. Physical Suicide of the Body leads to actual death of the body and cutting short God's purposes for very existence. This act is presumption. It attempts to ascend by self efforts to be like God. It is rebellious, prideful, lustful, and selfish because care is not given to whomever else it hurts (Hebrews 9:27).

ALL TYPES OF SUICIDE MUST BE CONFESSED, REPENTED OF, AND NAMED OUT LOUD (REJECTED) FOR DELIVERANCE. IN REJECTING SUICIDE AND ALL DEATH WISHES, YOU MUST ALSO CONFESS "LIFE" AND "A LOVE FOR LIFE". LIFE IS THE CHRISTIAN POSITION, A MOST UNIQUE AND WONDERFUL GIFT.

Here are some scriptures that bring into perspective the attitude God has toward this wasteful, rebellious act of suicide:

"..There among those nations (places where the believer does not belong, practicing idolatry) ..you will find no repose, no resting place for the sole of your foot. There the Lord will give you an anxious mind, eyes weary with longing, and a despairing heart. You will live in constant suspense, filled with dread both night and day, NEVER SURE OF YOUR LIFE. In the morning you will say, 'If only it were evening!' and in the evening, 'If only it were morning! ..There you will offer yourselves for sale to your enemies as male and female slaves, BUT NO ONE WILL BUY YOU." Dt 28:64-68.

"Yea, though I walk THROUGH THE VALLEY OF THE SHADOW OF DEATH, I will fear no evil: for thou art with me; thy rod and thy staff, they comfort me." Psalm 23:4 (KJV).

"Even in laughter the heart is sorrowful; and the end of that mirth, is heaviness." Pr 14:13 (KJV).

"I waited patiently for the Lord, and He inclined unto me and heard my cry. He brought me up OUT OF AN HORRIBLE PIT, OUT OF THE MIRY CLAY and set my feet upon a rock, and established my goings. And He put a new song in my mouth, even praise unto our God!" Ps 40:1-3 (KJV).

God is always near to deliver from the worse situations, even one close to your own death. Look at what he did for David in 1 and 2 Samuel and what he was saved from. REACH OUT FOR HELP. Take time to wait and listen to God's voice. Get away from your normal routine and sincerely give attention to the Lord. Let Him get you on the right path and give you a new song of real joy to praise Him with. It is a matter of believing Him to do it for you by acting on it.

The Tyrant Of Fear

In the Hebrew, *YARE* and *YIRAH* (the good, positive reverance "fear" of the Lord) is contrasted to *MORAH* and *MORA* meaning "to have dread, be terror-filled, a fearful deed or thing". *'EMAH* was another word used to connote "fright, an idol (as a bugbear); dread, fear, horror, anxiety, quaking, trembling, exceedingly crushed, dismayed, broken, afraid; to shutter (more or less violently)". While GUWR is "to turn aside, shrink from, fear (as in a strange place), to gather for hostility; abide, assemble to be afraid, dwell and sojourn in fear."

New Testament writers used the Greek words *EULABEIA* and *EULABEOMAI* meaning "to fear reverentially and with caution; to be circumspect, religiously reverent (pious), be apprehensive". This is the life-giving, positive side of fear.

Other New Testament words in contrast to positive fear are the negative words of *DEILIA* and *DEILOS:* "to be timid, fearful, faithless, and strange". *PHOBOS* and its companion word *PHEBOMAI* used elsewhere mean "to be put in fear of; exceedingly alarmed; a frightening thing, terrific portent, a fearful sight".

We see that fear is spoken of as positive—going toward God and as a negative—going toward the flesh, the world, and Satan. Negative, crippling fears arising from the human nature are not demonic and will disappear with the reading and affirmation of the Word, prayer, self-discipline (putting fear in its place by exchanging the fearful situation to become a place of faith), and through developing a Renewed Mind. Another positive type of fear is sensing danger and preserving your life and limb. We would not even survive all the pitfalls of childhood were it not for this God-given, natural fear of danger.

NEGATIVE FEAR IS NEGATIVE FAITH.
NEGATIVE FEAR MUST BE DISPLACED BY GODLY FAITH.

"Fear not" was a constant admonition of Jesus' to His disciples. It was spoken by God to His people over 360 times in the Bible. It seems, then, that fear can be easily introduced into a life that is not fixed upon the Lord or when one is faced by great stress, threat of bodily harm, or as a result of doing what is wrong.

Fear is one of the first emotions in evidence after the fall in the Garden of Eden. It plagued different men and women of God like Moses (fear to speak), Saul (feared the people), Abram (fear of remaining childless), Jacob (feared his brother would kill him), Ruth (feared famine, rejection, lack of provision) and the Apostle Paul (feared shipwreck and loss of life).

This kind of fear is negative and hinders trust and reliance on God to protect, care for and provide the necessities of the whole personality. Proverbs 29:25 (KJV) says, *"..the fear of man bringeth a snare."* These outstanding men and women did overcome their fears through God's provision and remain as examples to our generation as delivered overcomers. At those particularly crucial points in their lives they were paralyzed with fear until they let go, and let God.

Demonic spiritual fears invade to rob faith and faith-living. Its strength lies in hitting at our weakest moments with suggestions that seem bigger than life. Often the devilish suggestions prove more to reckon with than fear itself because suggestions are lies. Facts, however, prove Truth and never come from the pits of Hell.

When Fear suggestions are embraced, believed, and allowed to take root, another principle of God comes into effect found in Isaiah 66:3-4 *"..They have chosen their own ways, and their souls delight in their abominations; so I also will choose harsh treatment for them and WILL BRING UPON THEM WHAT THEY DREAD. For when I called, no one answered, when I spoke, no one listened. They did evil in my sight and chose what displeases me."*

Willful disobedience opens one up to fears and the very things feared WILL COME UPON YOU. It is like a lightening rod fastened to the highest peak of a roof, inviting lightening to strike. And sure enough, it does! Negative fear has no place at all in the Christian's personhood.

Fear is a great open door by which Satan enters to torment and can be either the strongman or a lesser demon who is invited by another strongmen-demon in search for unoccupied places. Jesus in Matthew 12:43-45, gave us much insight into the workings of displaced spirits. He said, *"When an evil spirit comes out of a man, it goes through arid places seeking rest and does not find it. Then it says, 'I will return to the house I left.' When it arrives, it finds the house unoccupied, swept clean and put in order. Then it goes and takes with it seven other spirits more wicked than itself, and they go in and live there..."*

Expressions of Fear

Fears are expressed in various ways and evil spirits use these expressions as points of vexation. Take these examples of guilt, doubts, condemnation, passivity, social timidity, suspicion, indecision, bondage, restlessness, shame, supersition, insecurity, superiority, worry, haughtiness, aggressiveness; over-education ("I need two more doctorates, just in case"), hoarding money, selfish use of possessions, the fear of man (peer pressure), suicide, loneliness, reticence to venture out, defiance to any authority figure, not exercising your own opinions, unreasonable denial, withholding sex from spouse.

Others include an unwillingness to participate in groups for prayer, fellowship, to complete projects or tasks. There are many, many fears that can be listed but you know your own most crippling and tiniest fears where the battle takes up and combat must be launched.

Another place fear expresses itself is in social attachments. There are Christians who will marry not for love or from obedience to God, but out of fear of loneliness and insecurity. The culmination of that union of misplaced faith is one of stealing a reliance on God to supply ALL needs by placing trust in a human person who should not and cannot meet most needs. What an insult to God and how dishonest to yourself and spouse.

People who are afraid to grow into adulthood never learn intimacy. They are most comfortable searching for 100% sure things bearing no risk. Fear causes Christians to bury their talents from a faulty consideration of other's opinions or from expecting failure instead of success. They are unsure of what is right and wrong, cannot take criticism or punishment for misdeeds, are manipulative and often small minded. Fear torments by doubt.

Fear is the motivating factor in overbearing, smothering parents who are afraid of losing their child and his or her love. These parents are determined to create fear in the child to keep them home, keep them from rough sports, from dating, or from getting on with any of the risks (and rewards) of coming into adulthood. I have spoken with many people who suffered from a controlling spirit of fear that had reached across the years into the child's own marriage causing pain and soul ties to be broken so that both parent and child could go into maturity as separate beings.

"Ye have FEARED THE SWORD, and I WILL BRING A SWORD UPON YOU, saith the Lord God." Ez 11:8 (KJV).

"..If you are determined to go to Egypt and you do go to settle there, then the sword YOU FEAR WILL OVERTAKE YOU THERE, and the famine YOU DREAD WILL FOLLOW YOU into Egypt, and there you will die." Jer 42:13-16.

"For the thing which I GREATLY FEARED is come upon me, and THAT WHICH I WAS AFRAID OF IS COME UNTO ME." Job 3:25 (KJV).

POSITIVE FAITH VERSES NEEDED
TO COMBAT FEAR:

"The FEAR OF THE LORD is the beginning of knowledge: but fools despise wisdom and instruction." Pr 1:7 (KJV).

"The FEAR OF THE LORD is to hate evil: pride, arrogancy, the evil way, and the froward mouth do I hate." Pr 9:10, 8:13 (KJV).

"God is our refuge and strength, a tested help in times of trouble. And SO WE NEED NOT FEAR EVEN IF THE WORLD BLOWS UP, and the mountains crumble into the sea." Ps 46:1-2 (LIV).

"It is the Lord who goes before you; He will (march) with you; He will not fail you nor forsake you; (let there be no cowardice or flinching, but FEAR NOT, NEITHER BECOME BROKEN (in spirit) (depressed, dismayed and unnerved with alarm)." Dt 31:8 (AMP).

"I sought the Lord, and He heard me, and DELIVERED ME FROM ALL MY FEARS." Ps 34:4 (KJV).

"There is NO FEAR IN LOVE; but PERFECT LOVE CASTETH OUT FEAR: because FEAR HATH TORMENT." 1 Jn 4:18 (KJV).

The Bible is literally filled with faith verses that can be quoted, memorized, and used as battle weapons against all kinds of fears. Negative fear is unreasonable so do not try to reason it out and understand it. Reject its intrusion into your mind and act in faith in these situations. God never brings fear. Humans do not seek or naturally act in fear. Satan is the master of fear.

As an example of someone speaking their fears onto you, should they say "Oh, you're allergic to cats". Don't accept that into your mind. By all means take precautions around anything seen to be harmful to a great many people, but DO NOT ASSUME a fear of allergy for yourself. Everyone is not allergic to cats.

Addictions And Double-mindedness

There is much in common with addictive behaviors and being double-minded, for both are used as coping mechanisms. In addiction, people are ensnared by the lusts of the pleasures of tobacco use, glue sniffing, marijuana, hard drugs, prescription drugs, alcohol, over-eating (bulimia) or under-eating (anorexia). They use substances out of vanity or fear and can become dependent on anything from rock music, the occultic and athletic excess to caffeine products. They may also adopt some compulsive behaviors such as incessant washing of the hands or sweeping, biting nails, illicit sex, or daily horoscope reading before stepping out the front door.

Under the seduction of addictive spirits evident in advertising for consumer addictive products, people are tempted with a half truth. Some "benefit" will be derived from taking up the addictive habit. For example, not so long ago it was considered "sophisticated" to smoke tobacco products. Then science found links to cancer.

Likewise, drug pushers seduce with the philosophy of "get as many highs out of life as possible". Millions have been initiated into alcoholism by the pressure to "be a part of the crowd and your social equals—drink" Athletes are not immune to these ploys either and are taunted with "run until you 'hit the wall' to feel the runner's high".

And of course, we have all heard the little devils whisper, "Go ahead. horoscopes can't hurt you—they're just fun". How many cups of coffee. coke, or tea have you had thinking it will just "calm your nerves"? Or the abuse of prescriptive drugs with the idea implanted these pills can "only help" you. However, these are deceptive lies from Satan, the father of lies setting the bait higher and the trap steeper by encasing it in worldly sayings.

WHAT YOU CANNOT CONQUER HAS CONQUERED YOU.

Regarding being double-minded, the Hebrew for this is taken from the very interesting word KAPHAL, "to fold together, duplicate, double, bend, and repeat" (Ps 12:2). New Testament Greek for the same word is *DISTAZO* or *DISPUCHOS* meaning "twice, to duplicate, waver in opinion, have doubt; be two-spirited (vacillating in opinion and purpose) and of two minds." Double-mindedness is idolatry.

Counselors, how do you recognize a double-minded person who comes to you for help? Perhaps they don't even know this is a trait although they are suffering from the confusion it genders. It is characterized by someone thinking and expressing themself in one way but reacting from the emotions or another part of the soul in a completely different way refuting the first process. A dual personality can be created with much of one personality demonic in origin having been given over totally to Satan.

As in allowing addictive disorders to rule a life, so being double-minded can lead to serious physical and mental diseases. From a demonic viewpoint, one or multiple (legion) spirits can enter a person (usually at great crises like rejection, denial of the death of a loved one, pain beyond the threshold of bearance, or through traumatic childhood experiences), to create conflicting and confusing thoughts.

The afflicted may actually hear voices, see things, and react as if the world inside were as real or more so, than life. They may be mild or violent in nature but will experience a definite disturbance and a distortion within the personality (whole man). In these instances, it is essential for prayer counselors to begin at the point of salvation before any deliverance is possible.

Some mental illness is physical and genetic in character and needs prayer for a miracle of healing and not necessarily deliverance while under medical care. Do not ever advise people to stop or change medication or direct ANY medical activity. That is the medical practitioner's place, certainly not the prayer counselor's responsibility.

Addictive habits must be broken under the power of the Blood of Jesus Christ. Counsel them to ernestly seek God for forgiveness and deliverance and never go back to the addiction again. Pray for God TO HEAL ANY PHYSICAL DAMAGE AS A RESULT OF THE ADDICTIVE BEHAVIOR after deliverance is complete.

Some diabolical spirits that may reside with double-mindedness, addiction, and the results of addictive habits are: fear of man, hallucigens, hallucinations, disease, cancers, emphysema, asthma, brain damage, confusion, conflict, calamity, double-personality, lust of the flesh, insecurity, egoism, self-pity, death, torture, self-denial, schizophrenia, martyr-spirit, sensationalism, flamboyance, nervousness, hatred, hiding-out, a childish spirit ("I can't make up my mind"), pouting, instability, deceit, division, hypocrite, unclean spirits, flagellation (beating or abusing the body), pride, and more.

"But when he asks, he must BELIEVE AND NOT DOUBT, because he who doubts is like a wave of the sea, blown and tossed by the wind. That man should not think he will receive anything from the Lord; HE IS A DOUBLE-MINDED MAN, UNSTABLE IN ALL HE DOES." Ja 1:6-8; 4:7-10.

"Their heart is divided: now shall they be found faulty." Ho 10:2 "KJV).

"Some became fools through their rebellious ways and SUFFERED AFFLICTION because of their iniquities. They LOATHED ALL FOOD AND DREW NEAR TO THE GATES OF DEATH." Ps 107:17-20.

"Woe to those who are wise in their own eyes and clever in their own sight." Is 5:21.

"I (Paul) eagerly EXPECT AND HOPE that I will IN NO WAY BE ASHAMED, but will have sufficient courage so that now as always CHRIST WILL BE EXALTED IN MY BODY, whether by life or by death." Phil 1:20.

"Know ye not that they which run in a race run all, BUT ONE receiveth the prize? So run, that ye may obtain. And every man that striveth for mastery IS TEMPERATE IN ALL THINGS..I keep under my body, and BRING IT INTO SUBJECTION lest that by any means, when I have preached to others, I myself should be a castaway." 1 Co 9:24-27 (KJV).

"Pride, lust, and evil actions ARE ALL SIN." Pr 21:4 (KJV).

"Peace I leave with you: my peace I GIVE YOU. I do not give to you as the world gives. Do not let your hearts be troubled and DO NOT BE AFRAID." Jn 14:27.

"For GOD HATH NOT GIVEN US THE SPIRIT OF FEAR; but of power, and of love, and of a sound mind." 2 Ti 1:7 (KJV).

"Blessed are the PURE IN HEART for they shall see God." Mt 5:8 (KJV). NOTE: there is no mixture or double spirit here, but only purity.

The next chapter will deal directly with receiving deliverance. These last several chapters were designed to give a background in becoming equipped to understand the basic areas of bondage and how to be on the watch for invading spirits, negative attitudes, and the willful acceptance and tolerance of suggestions to sin. Praise our God that He is ready, willing, and so very able to deliver us from all oppressive circumstances through the liberation and renewal of a pure spirit!

CHAPTER 8

How To Receive Your Deliverance

It is difficult to comprehend the magnitude of what deliverance is and what it means. People who are being vexed and oppressed only know that they are very uncomfortable and in difficult and life-threatening bondage. They want to be free. They must be free to go on. And the beauty, the provision, the health that results from God on behalf of His child is startling when that freedom comes.

We will begin to understand in part by seeing the original meanings for the words deliverance, delivering, delivers, and deliverer occuring in Scripture about 630 times. It is a powerful word of "exchange" that dominated the experiences of the Jewish nation and later, the early Church. Before the Cross, a constant effort on God's part was made to keep His people delivered from their enemies, their own ill devices, and the devil's schemes. After the Cross, it was a different story.

Today deliverance is a finished fact by Christ's perfect sacrifice. It is the child of God's by spiritual inheritance but like any legacy, we must go into enemy territory to lay hold of it. Deliverance from demonic oppression does not just happen. And keeping delivered and free from spiritual interference is a concentrated and consecrated effort on the believer's part.

Praise God we know that all the powers of God by the unceasing vigilance of the Holy Spirit are at the back of the active resistance of the man or woman determined to remain cleansed and free of all hell's minions.

"So whoever cleanses himself (from what is ignoble and unclean)—WHO SEPARATES HIMSELF FROM CONTACT WITH CONTAMINATING AND CORRUPTING INFLUENCES—will (then himself) be a vessel set apart and useful for honorable and noble purposes, consecrated and profitable to the Master, FIT AND READY FOR ANY GOOD WORK." 2 Ti 2:21 (AMP).

There are at least 20 words denoting deliverance in Hebrew. Here are several. *GA'AL* means to "redeem, to be the next of kin, to buy back a relative's property, avenger; deliverer, kinsfolk, purchaser, ransom, revenger." *CHALATS* is a word with a different connotation meaning to "pull off; to strip, depart, deliver and equip for fight; be present to strengthen; arm (self), go, ready armed, draw out, make fat, loose, prepared, take away, withdraw."

YASHA and *Y'SHUWAH* have companion root meanings of "something saved, deliverance; hence aid, victory, prosperity, health, help, salvation, saving health, welfare; to preserve, rescue, bring (having) salvation, to be open, wide or free (be safe), succor."

Several other Hebrew words are *MALAT,* "to escape as by slipperiness, release or rescue smoothly, leap out, let alone, let go speedily and surely." And *MACAR,* to "sunder, set apart and apostatize; commit." *MAGAN* is to "shield, encompass with, to hand safely over and surrender to." *NATSAL* and *NATHAN* denote an aggressive deliverance of "to snatch away, spoil, escape without fail, pluck away; direct, distribute, let out, trade, weep and sing". Much of this concerns physical safety.

'ABAR brings out the transition aspect of deliverance by its meaning "to cause to cross over, overcome, overrun, make partition, cause to give over, a sweet smelling." And one last Hebrew word, *SHUWB,* uses threat and resistance by its action to "say nay, back off, recompense, recall, refresh, break, build, circumcise, dig out; to finish."

What a richness of meaning and provision God had for His people Israel. He used all means and methods to deliver then and how they needed it! The arm of the Lord was bared uncountable times on behalf of His beloved. Yet God provided a different way for His Bride, the Chruch.

The New Testament contains 16 different words for deliverance. Most of these are recorded during the period before the Cross exchange in Jesus' three-year earthly ministry placing it "under the law". Deliverance in the Old Testament sense was sought after three times as much as by Christians of the early Church age. Something had happened to lessen the need for deliverance after the victory of Calvary. It had become a work and walk of personal salvation as the Greek word roots denote.

Here are some Greek words for deliverance. *APOLUTROSIS* is to "ransom in full, have riddance, salvation, redemption". *DIDOMI* is more forceful: "to make, minister, have power, receive, set, smite or strike with the palm of the hand; take utterly, to yield". It takes an offensive position in deliverance by going forth from a war-stance as does *KATARGEO* by "pulling down, to make void and with none effect; put in prison".

CHARIZOMAI is a more conciliatory form of deliverance meaning to "grant as a favor gratuitously, in kindness, pardon or rescue; to deliver and frankly forgive and freely grant deliverance." *APHESIS* is another loving word that speaks of "freedom, forgiveness, liberty, and remission".

Deliverance from demonic influence, torment, and possession (with demons) is not only available, but fully funded. It is given freely and lovingly from the resources of our Heavenly Father. There are no special formulae or sets of rules. Deliverance into full freedom and spiritual prosperity simply begins with the whole-hearted intention of going on in God as a clean and fit vessel. The entire provision for it was deposited in the Christian's account at salvation.

How do we make the withdrawal? First of all let us discount all the areas according the God's Word we already know to be His will in order to stay out of bondage. Have you:

1) Tried to be free of evil by committing your life to Christ?
2) Been water baptized as a public testimony of your faith in obedience to God's Word?
3) Stayed in the Word for God to speak to you and obeyed what He has told you?
4) Fasted (Is 58:6) and prayed over your problem (Heb 4:16)?
5) Been counseled by a spiritual director or pastor?
6) Repented of and forgiven all others?

If you are still in torment and can't seem to break through to victory, it is likely you should submit yourself to intercessory prayer for deliverance. When the Lord leads and assures you of being in the right place to get intercessory prayer you will have the freedom to give yourself totally to God. Proverbs 28:13 (KJV) says, *"He who conceals his sins does not prosper, but whoever confesses and renounces them finds mercy."*

The very essence of deliverance deals with the person's sin of CHOOSING DEATH OVER LIFE. God will not and cannot intrude Himself onto you. Satan and all his hosts cannot push themselves on the Christian. The devil did not make you sin. God did not cause you to sin. YOU made the choice to enjoy the pleasures of sin for a season rather than follow God. That opened the door to evil.

This is why Repentance (turning yourself completely away from sin), Renouncing (taking back from Satan any legal rights you allowed him), and Renewal (going on with God in a new direction) are needed. Had God failed you or Satan run over you against your will, then THEY would need deliverance, not YOU.

"Rid yourselves of all the offenses you have committed, and get a new heart and a new spirit." Ez 18:31.

"Repent, then, and turn to God, so that your sins may be wiped out, that times of refreshing may come from the Lord." Ac 3:19.

"Wherefore, my beloved, as ye have always obeyed..WORK OUT YOUR OWN SALVATION with fear and trembling. For IT IS GOD WHICH WORKETH IN YOU both to will and do of His good pleasure." Phil 2:12-13 (KJV).

These verses testify that deliverance was given fully at the time of Salvation; IT IS SALVATION. "Working it out" means to avail yourself of it in its fullest sense—healing, freedom from obeying the flesh, victory over Satan, not tasting (spiritual) death, experiencing prosperity, fruitfulness, peace, joy; dedicating your life to Godly works and completing your purposes on earth. Working is active: you cannot sit in a heap and be showered with everything salvation means. You must take it. And taking back all the ground you have allowed Satan, is part of working out your salvation.

"For God hath not called us unto uncleanness, but unto holiness." 1 Th 4:7 (KJV).

In the areas where ancestral bondage, curses from without, and ignorance (e.g., use of the occult) are true in you, intercessory prayer with a team of those called to this ministry will prove very helpful in breaking these chains to gain freedom. Anyone seeking deliverance counseling must come in humility and openness with honesty and a total willingness to allow God to work. They must not lie to the Holy Spirit. And they should have confidence in God for whomever He chooses to minister through.

"Whoso offereth praise glorifieth me: and to him (or her) who orders his conversation (conduct) aright, WILL I SHOW THE SALVATION OF GOD." Ps 50:23 (KJV).

The Name and Blood of Jesus Christ Delivers

There are various ways for the team and counselees to become prepared to minister and receive deliverance. Some of these include prayer, praising

Chapter 8

the Lord, having the presence of godly music and entering into spiritual worship. Each are very powerful in inviting the presence of the Holy Spirit and His angelic army to assist and fight against the powers of darkness and entering into the Spirit for this operation. It also tunes human spirits into the voice and presence of God to bring readiness to receive from Him.

Worshipping in love, making restitution for sin (Mt 5:23-26), water and Spirit baptism, intercession on your behalf, fasting, repeating the confession of faith aloud, forgiving others, and experiencing physical healing are all ways to see God's deliverance begin to take place. There is no set way to pick and choose method possible. God moves sovereignly.

But the most powerful weapons in the accomplishment of this warfare is use of the Blood and Name of Jesus Christ. These two positions in the Spirit are our legal credentials for binding, breaking, and casting out all the evil influences of Satan and his minions.

"And these signs will accompany those who believe: IN MY NAME they will drive out demons..." Mk 16:17.

"Therefore God exalted him to the highest place and gave him the NAME THAT IS ABOVE EVERY NAME. That at the NAME OF JESUS every knee should bow, IN HEAVEN AND ON EARTH, AND UNDER THE EARTH." Phil 2:9-10.

"And I will do WHATEVER YOU ASK IN MY NAME, so that the Son may bring glory to the Father. You may ask me for anything IN MY NAME, and I will do it." Jn 14:13-14.

"Salvation (deliverance) is found in no one else, FOR THERE IS NO OTHER NAME under heaven given to men BY WHICH WE MUST BE SAVED." Acts 4:12 and 19:13-17.

"..because FOR HIS NAME'S SAKE your sins are forgiven—pardoned through HIS NAME AND ON ACCOUNT OF CONFESSING HIS NAME." 1 Jn 2:12 (AMP).

"And there was war in heaven. Michael and his angels fought against the dragon, and the dragon and his angels fought back. But he WAS NOT STRONG ENOUGH, and they lost their place in heaven. The great dragon was hurled down—that ancient serpent called the devil, or Satan, who leads the whole world astray. He was

hurled to the earth, and his angels with him.

"Then I heard a loud voice in heaven say: 'Now have come the salvation and power and the kingdom of our God and THE AUTHORITY OF HIS CHRIST. For the accuser of our brothers, who accuses them before our God day and night, has been hurled down. THEY OVERCAME HIM BY THE BLOOD OF THE LAMB AND BY THE WORD OF THEIR TESTIMONY; they did not love their lives so much as to shrink from death. Therefore, REJOICE, you heavens, and you who dwell in them!" Re 12:7-12.

"..whom God set forth to be a propitiation BY HIS BLOOD, THROUGH FAITH, to demonstrate His righteousness, because in His forbearance God had passed over the sins that were previously committed." Ro 3:25 (NKJ).

"Therefore, brethren, having boldness to enter the Holiest BY THE BLOOD OF JESUS." He 10:19 (NKJ).

"How much more, then, will the BLOOD OF CHRIST.. CLEANSE OUR CONSCIENCES FROM ACTS THAT LEAD TO DEATH, so that we may serve the living God!" He 9:14 (NKJ).

"..the BLOOD OF JESUS CHRIST His Son, CLEANSES (REMOVES) US FROM ALL SIN AND GUILT..keeps us cleansed from sin in ALL ITS FORMS and MANIFESTATIONS." 1 Jn 1:7 (AMP).

The Spoken Word of God Delivers

Speaking out for your deliverance is evidence that you want deliverance. It is activating faith and is, itself, active faith. FAITH is what moves your mountains and you only need a measure of it the size of a tiny mustard seed. The Lord tells us to CHOOSE THIS DAY WHETHER YOU WANT LIFE OR DEATH. And, *"Death and life are in the power of the tongue: and they that love it shall eat the fruit thereof"* (Pr 18:21).

Renouncing out loud by speaking, coughing, yawning, spitting, or by any other physical manisfestation during deliverance facilitates demonic removal. Some counselees have these reactions, others do not. But should you feel to do or use physical reactions to reject demons, it is encouraged and is in order. Counselors may ask you to assist in your own deliverance in these ways. Submit and be open.

> *"When the even was come, they brought unto him many that were possessed with devils: and HE CAST OUT THE SPIRITS WITH HIS WORD, and He healed all that were sick."* Mt 8:16 (KJV).

> *"The centurion replied, 'Lord, I do not deserve to have you come under my roof. But just SAY THE WORD, and my servant will be healed'. (Jesus said)..'I tell you the truth, I have not found anyone in Israel with such great faith...Go! it will be done JUST AS YOU BELIEVED IT WOULD.' And his servant was healed at that very hour."* Mt 8:8-13.

> *"In the beginning was the Word, and the Word was with God, and THE WORD WAS GOD."* Jn 1:1 (KJV).

> *"For with the heart man believeth unto righteousness; and WITH THE MOUTH CONFESSION is made unto salvation (DELIVERANCE)."* Ro 10:10 (KJV).

Prayer For Deliverance

Intercessory prayer counselors under the guidance of the Holy Spirit and with the authority of the spiritual head of Jesus Christ will "stand in the gap and build up the wall" (Eze 22:30) for counselees during deliverance. Prayer counselors are usually teamed in twos or threes, will have back-up prayer warriors, may have fasted and prayed with and/or for you beforehand, and are engifted with various gifts of the Holy Spirit for this ministry.

One of these specific gifts is the Word of Knowledge (discernment of spirits) whereby God reveals the exact nature of the problem, the demons, their names and activities. While the one being prayed for needs to be open, it is not necessary for him or her to either reveal or delve into unedifying details of sin. The Lord can deliver by just the name of the spirit(s) who are molesting. Also, calling for the names of demons to manifest themselves is inviting a lie. Depend on the Holy Spirit to answer the truth by the Word of Knowledge and believe by faith that deliverance is accomplished.

Other gifts of the Spirit used in this ministry are the Word of Wisdom and Exhortation so the person prayed for witnesses in his or her own spirit to the truth of what is happening, and is encouraged thereby. Other gifts may be Diversities of Tongues (warring prayer languages), Faith, Healing, and Miracles. There may be other gifts and callings as God determines in each case. Bathed in this atmosphere will be the Spirit of unity, love, forgiveness, healing and reconciliation and restoration.

Prayer Counselors in no wise reveal any confidential remarks made during the deliverance sessions outside this circle of prayer. They are not alarmed by any confession, are not critical, judgmental, or condemnatory. They are merely God's "stand-in", with all prayers and praise going out to the Father and left in that room when you are finished.

"And the servant of the Lord must not strive; but be gentle unto all, apt to teach, patient. In meekness instructing THOSE THAT OPPOSE THEMSELVES; if God peradventure will give them repentance to the acknowledging of the truth; AND THAT THEY MAY RECOVER THEMSELVES OUT OF THE SNARE OF THE DEVIL, who are taken captive by him at his (own) will." 2 Tim 2:24-27.

The following steps may be taken by the one needing prayer if they are alone or with prayer counselors if available. These are suggestions only. Please understand that there is FULL LIBERTY in each session to deal AS THE LORD WISHES in each case. Be prepared to spend some extended time in deliverance with the possibility that everything cannot be done in one sitting and various appointed times might be needed.

PLACING ON THE ARMOR OF GOD

---

1. Praise and Worship God. Pray to seek God's complete control and guidance.

2. Pray the following prayer to put on the whole armor of God as taken from Ephesians 6:10-18. It is helpful for both counselors and counselee to pray this together:

"Lord, we are strong in You and in Your mighty power by our position in the beloved. Right now, in the name of your only begotten Son, Jesus the Christ, we put on Your full armor to take our stand against the devil's schemes for we know that this struggle today is not against flesh and blood in human terms, but it is against the spiritual rulers, authorities and evil powers of this dark world and against all the spiritual forces of evil in the heavenly realms.

"Therefore, Oh God, we are standing our ground and reclaiming lost ground to the enemy by putting on the BELT OF TRUTH: it is buckled on our waists. And we put on the BREASTPLATE OF RIGHTEOUSNESS. Our feet are now fitted with the readiness that comes from the GOSPEL OF PEACE. In addition to all this, we are taking up the SHIELD OF FAITH with which You can extinguish ALL the flaming arrows of the evil one. We put on by faith, the HELMET OF SALVATION AND DELIVERANCE and take the SWORD OF THE SPIRIT which is the WORD OF GOD.

"Lord, we are ready and alert to see You battle this day and on Your children's behalf. We anticipate a great victory for Your name's sake. We praise You, O mighty God and Father. We praise You, Jesus Christ, our only Deliverer. And we praise You, Holy Spirit, our Comforter. AMEN SO BE IT LORD."

BINDING THE STRONGMAN

3. Bind the Strongman of the house so you may go in and take back what he took over. This keeps him from bringing harm and destruction (Mt 12:29, 18:18-19, Lk 11:21-22, Jn 20:23). Repeat this together out loud:

"By the Name and Blood of Jesus Christ, we bind you Satan, all your demons, and all your powers over _____(use counselee's full name here), a born-again child of God. We bind you in the air above, in the earth below, in the waters around, and in the netherworld. You are a liar and the father of lies and you do not possess or own any territory in _____. (use counselee's full name here.) We have put on the full armor of God and agree together to take dominion over you in this life. We bind you from influencing, harming, or entering any person or object in or without this place. You are commanded by the power of Jesus Christ, to go where His Spirit directs you, wandering in the dessert places. We hereby plead over each of us the protective Blood of the Lamb of God, the Lord Jesus Christ, who defeated Satan at Calvary. Praise God. We believe it is done! AMEN."

THE CONFESSION OF FAITH

4. A confession of faith, out loud, is made by the person coming for

deliverance. Here follows an example: however, you are free to use your own words. A confession of faith establishes within the counselee's own mind his or her rights and standing as a child of God.

"Dear Lord Jesus, I am Your child. I fully trust you for my salvation from sin and its consequences. Thank you for dying for my sin and bringing me into Your family. My testimony is that God gave me eternal life and this life is in His Son Jesus Christ who came in the flesh. I believe that Jesus Christ is the only begotten Son of God, and give ALL my allegiance, my life, and my love to Him. I ask you now Lord Christ, to be the only Lord of my life. And because of this confession, I now take back every bit of ground that was given over to Satan and to every evil spirit. AMEN."

5. With the first four steps completed, begin deliverance by having the person CONFESS any known areas of sin, then REPENT of them, and RENOUNCE them. If there is no one thing that is pressing the counselee, a good place to start is in the area of the occult. Take the list given in this manual in Appendix III and repent and renounce EACH one. Read them all even if some are unfamiliar and add others if known. Satan knows what territory he occupies.

6. Next for deliverance to take place in specific areas, forgiveness must be given to all and everyone who has ever harmed, offended, rejected, defeated, or set themselves against you as an enemy. This includes family members, friends, business associates, spouse, children, ex-spouses, ex-relatives, ex-business people, and the like.

You may need to forgive organizations that are racial, political, legal, medical, the government, church people and pastors, roommates, schoolmates, anyone who ever had power or authority over you or been under your authority, the Draft Board or recruiters. Forgive those who have given you bad advice that was financial or psychological. Forgive any criminal behavior against you, abortionists, cheaters and those who have stolen from you. Anyone, no matter how remote the possibility (even those whom you cannot remember names for), must be forgiven in the Name of Jesus.

God will bring many names to your mind at this time. Be open and take your time. Say each out loud and then forgive them out loud by an act of your will. You don't have to feel anything to forgive someone. It is an obedient step of faith and act of the will. Be prepared to spend some time doing this. FORGIVING THEM FOR HARMING YOU RELEASES YOU TO GO FREE OF THEIR INFLUENCE OVER YOU.

7. Do the same as Step Six for all whom YOU have hated, resented, or have done harm to. Ask forgiveness of God for those you have offended and caused to stumble. BEING FORGIVEN OF YOUR OFFENSES RELEASES THEM TO GO FREE OF YOUR INFLUENCE AND GIVES GOD GROUND TO WORK WITH IN THEM.

8. Confess all your unconfessed sins. This is where you loose the specific tentacles of rebellion and idolatry. Some other areas to consider—as they apply—are homosexuality, religious perversions, strife, hate, fear, abortion, arson, crimes against man and God, lying, stealing, leading others astray, hurts, bribery, self-pity, domination, addictive habits, bitterness, murmuring, criticism, depression, mental illness, control, jezebel, ahab, lusts, love of disease, loneliness, manipulation, guilt, anxiety, suicide, murder, unbelief, passivity, immaturity, despair, adultery, bestiality, incest, phobias, pride, ego, drug abuse, revenge, body abuse, verbal abuse, gossip, slander, undermining, double-mindedness, indecision, shyness, insecurity, seduction, stubbornness, resentment, deceitfulness, love of the world, materialism, vain philosophies, love of money, selfishness, malice, impatience, impudence, anger, violence, warring, contempt, mockery, greed, shouting, sarcasm, selfish ambition, lust of the eyes, body fixation, concealing sins, and all other sins God brings to mind.

9. Next is to deal with soul ties and curses over you and your family by breaking them in the mightly Name of Christ. If the first eight steps have taken much time, it might serve to schedule another appointment for seeking the Lord to reveal these areas to you. Otherwise, the prayer counselors will hear from the Lord and continue to reveal the curses and/or soul ties.

10. Always finish a deliverance session with a season of grateful praise for all the victories won on your behalf. Pray for a fresh baptism in the Holy Spirit and the placement of Himself in all those root canals and crevices swept and left clean with the vacating of Satan and his demons.

Just as a good army positions additional soldiers and equipment around a conquered area, so must the Christian walk in his and her deliverance experience. The immediate feelings of freedom and love after a deliverance session goes a long way in refreshing those delivered but God calls you higher. That call consists of keeping the deliverance on a day by day basis. For this reason, the next chapter is included and should be a reference point to return to again and again as the victories become an integral part of the liberated and God-centered nature.

CHAPTER 9

Keeping Your Deliverance Fresh

Deliverance from the power of Satan was instant under the hand of Jesus Christ when He ministered. Certain people with faith and hope for renewal continually chased after Christ to recieve that divine touch that forever left them changed. They knew they had met the Master. Then the Cross happened and eternal changes became possible. But it happened one day at a time. Just like it happens to every one who ever walked Christ's way into freedom. How do we keep that freshness after the touch of Jesus in deliverance?

Changing human behavior patterns that have developed on paths once wrongly traveled, is tough. Keeping to God's pathway of His will takes effort and sincerity. But this is the way of blessing and God's favor. Remember, the NORMAL Christian life is one of HEARING God's voice to you and OBEYING IT.

You will find that doing so will be contrary to everything you can see, feel, hear, or think is "right" from how you used to walk in the world system. Now, you live by faith and faith never uses the physical senses or human intellect. It is the "cross life" that will keep you refreshed in the Renewed Mind of Christ.

SECTION I—Walking In The Holy Spirit

There once was a servant who climbed the ladder of life. He worked very hard, was sincere, good, and endeavored to be a success in life. After 72 years of climbing he got to the top. What an effort! He was very proud because he had never stopped once, never gotten off his ladder, honed in on his goal for success and even climbed in hardship times. At the top he paused and looked around into misty darkness.

He was startled at what he saw. It was at this long awaited moment that he realized he had placed his well-intentioned ladder against the wrong wall! Over to the right were other servants simply walking with great ease up prepared stairways. Some of them looked fairly battered, but the light they were climbing into was so glorious. They were loaded down with fruit, crowns, rewards, and happiness. He felt despair, then panic.

But what about him? Along the way he earned fine clothing, real estate and hoards of gold. He had so much he built bigger warehouses to hold it all. Now, at the top, he had not one possession. Surely it was too late to begin climbing again—even if he could find the right stairway. It would take another 72 years to get down his ladder just to begin afresh. He would be long dead. Too late. And how sincere he had been.

One thing this sorry and unfaithful servant learned too late was that those who follow Christ by faith do not choose their ladders of life. They do not select which walls to lean them against. There is no human control over how tall or how short or how sturdy their ladders are. They cannot control what country or race or economic position to be born into to begin the climb. That all happens by the sovereign will of God.

This ladder is the specific, individual and personalized cross each believer bears through life. No one has one exactly like another's—not throughout all the ages. It might be rugged. It might be smooth. But one thing is certain, no one can climb it on self-effort and expect anything but the Lord's rebuke at the end.

The cross life is death to everything the self desires, esteems, and admires. The cross that God has for you is unique: it is designed to work against your carnal nature so that out of the dry, hard bulb of life, you will grow as a strong planting of the Lord fully able to fruit in your timing and place.

As if it were not hard enough to avoid the landslides and pitfalls in an evil world within which the foot of your ladder stands, Satan untiredly waits for opportunities to pull up the roots of your soul. He puts all his forces together to allow the canker and palmer worms eat at your most tender blossoms. And every effort possible is made to delay or destroy the fruition of your spirit that will bless others.

The good news is that some Christians who have doggedly kept to His path are able to come to bloom many times—even a hundredfold—and find comfort in the cross Christ gave them. They have learned to "count it all joy" and go on anyway. Despite what you may feel about your cross, out of it comes blessing and life.

The Cross Life

Salvation (deliverance, healing, peace, God's love) is free and freely given, but it is not cheap. Never cheap. It took too much from Jesus Christ throughout the ages—and especially during His walk on earth—for us to disdain and abuse that grace in careless and heedless living.

Dietrich Bonhoffer, a martyred young man of 36, was killed just days before the allies arrived to liberate prisoners from Hitler's death camps in 1945. Even in this most unlikely of gardens God caused him to bloom in solitary confinement, under torture, humiliation, and starvation in order to write a classic model on *The Cost of Discipleship.* He clearly explains the cross that is laid on every Christian and what a privilege it is to walk in its discipline. It is still in print and suggested reading.

Bonhoffer explained about the Christ-suffering every person must experience as a call to abandon the attachments of the world in order to encounter Christ. It is in this discipleship we learn to surrender our lives unto death. When Christ calls a person, he bids them come and die (to the self-life). But we do not want to die even though we realize that this call of Christ in His baptism is what sets the Christian into the very middle of the daily arena against sin and the devil. New temptations, trials, and sufferings create the wounds and scars received in the combat of obedience as living tokens of participation in the cross of the Lord.

There is another kind of suffering and shame which Bonhoffer says Christians are not spared from. It is undergoing hardship in order to bear the sins of others. This can only be done through the strength of Christ to overcome their sins. How? It is accomplished by forgiving them their trespasses against you.

That is how the believer becomes the bearer of other men's burdens (Gal 6:2). Our duty to the law of Christ is this bearing of our particular cross which will, from time to time, include forgiving our brother's and sister's sins against us. And the only way to bear that sin is by the power of the cross of Christ in which we now gladly share.

Therefore, the call to follow Christ always means a call to share in the work of forgiving others their sins. Forgiveness is the Christlike suffering which is the Christian's duty and privilege to bear. That is why forgiveness glues deliverance together as an ongoing grace. It is because we may continue to sin as a part of the unregenerated nature and because others will continually need that forgiveness to be freed from their own bondage.

Chapter 9

SECTION II—Hearing And Obeying God's Voice

Keeping your deliverance, just like every Christian keeps their deliverance, means to daily come under the discipline of hearing and obeying God's voice. As you are clean and free and continue to become free, the promise of the Holy Spirit becomes more real. He is within to help you hear and obey God's voice so you learn to make godly choices and give no ground to Satan, the flesh, or the world. It is learning to operate from your own spirit in response to His wishes and not "solving the problem" out of the intellect, will, or emotions.

The Biblical guidelines given below will help to recognize God's voice and distinguish it from the world's voices. Once you are keyed in to obeying His ways, learning His character, and understanding His methods of assisting and discipling His children, you will be traveling the Path. Your ladder will be on the right wall and it won't be knocked out from under you. The apostle James admonishes us with, *"Do not merely listen to the word, and so deceive yourselves. Do what it says."* (James 1:22).

1. God Speaks When You are in a Position to Hear

"Therefore brothers, we have an obligation—but it is not to the sinful nature, to live according to it. For if you live according to the sinful nature, you will die; but if by the Spirit you put to death the misdeeds of the body, you will live, because those who are led by the Spirit of God are sons of God. For you did not receive a spirit that makes you a slave again to fear, but you received the Spirit of sonship. And by him we cry, 'Abba, Father'. THE SPIRIT HIMSELF TESTIFIES WITH OUR SPIRIT that we are God's children. Now if we are children, then we are heirs—heirs of God and co-heirs with Christ, IF INDEED WE SHARE IN HIS SUFFERINGS in order that we may also share in his glory." Ro 8:12-17.

"Then the man and his wife HEARD the sound of the Lord God as he was walking in the garden in the cool of the day, and they hid from the Lord God among the trees of the garden. But the Lord God called to the man, 'WHERE ARE YOU?' " Ge 3:8-9.

I want to add just a word regarding this last reference in Genesis. Adam and Eve were in a position of hearing God (they were still His children even after their disobedience), but instead of facing Him, they chose to break fellowship and hide. Of course no one can hide from God. But out of love the Lord called to them, "Where are you?" Just so, the Lord continues to give us opportunities to turn back to Him after disobedience. Hearing God's voice is important; but if after you know His voice and try to hide by not obeying it, greater condemnation comes for knowing better and still choosing your own way.

2. God Speaks Through His Written Word

Disciplined time in the Word of God cannot be over-emphasized. MAKE a time and a special place where you can simply read the Bible every day. Do not take up this special time with other books about the Bible, but read the Word alone. Begin where you are comfortable (I like the Gospels to see how Jesus did it) and keep to your time schedule. If you don't seem to be getting anything from the reading stop and ask God to direct you. Be flexible and press on until the Lord has shown you something living for today.

If you still have trouble understanding the Word, in the Name of Jesus bind the spirit of blindness to the Word. Invite the Holy Spirit to quicken the Word to your spirit. Be open to literally believe what the passage is saying. Don't change it around to support what you already "feel" is truth. Renewal means change from the old so change your mind to literally believing what the Word is saying so you may act on it in confidence. This is your special, private time to open up to God. Go slowly and be persistent in understanding it.

It is out of disciplined time and devotion to receiving from the Lord that the washing of the Word over your mind will renew it. Soon you will be hearing the Lord in the very ordinary things of life. You will begin to see Him everywhere. Afterall, if God is not all around, how much harder it is to find Him in the stained-glass chapels human hands have fashioned.

"..just as Christ loved the church and gave Himself up for her, to make her holy, cleansing her by the WASHING WITH WATER THROUGH THE WORD, and to present her to Himself as a radiant church, without stain or wrinkle or any other blemish, but holy and blameless." Eph 5:25-27.

3. God Speaks Through His Nature and Will

Walking with God in holiness will open up a whole new relationship with Him you never thought possible. He is a personality, has a loving character, and moves in His own particular and stedfast ways. HE WANTS US TO KNOW WHO HE IS. That is part of His nature.

This next passage from Proverbs brings out God's willingness for us to go after the wisdom we need to walk the Christian life. It is not spoon-fed to us. We must look for it as hard as if trying to find sunken treasure. Someone (you) has got to hire the boat, drop the nets, and haul them aboard again in order to lay hold of that priceless treasure...but oh, the rewards!

> *"My son, if you accept my words and store up my commands within you, TURNING YOUR EAR to wisdom and APPLYING YOUR HEART to understanding, and if you call out for insight and cry aloud for understanding, and if you look for it as for silver and search for it as for hidden treasure, THEN you will understand the fear of the Lord and find the knowledge of God. For the Lord gives wisdom, and FROM HIS MOUTH come knowledge and understanding. He holds victory in store for the upright, he is a shield to those WHOSE WALK IS BLAMELESS, for He guards the COURSE of the just and protects THE WAY of his faithful ones.*
>
> *"THEN YOU WILL UNDERSTAND WHAT IS RIGHT AND JUST AND FAIR—EVERY GOOD PATH. For wisdom will enter your heart, and knowledge will be pleasant to your soul. Discretion will protect you, and understanding will guard you. Wisdom will save you from the ways of wicked men, from men whose words are perverse, who LEAVE THE STRAIGHT PATHS to walk in dark ways, who delight in doing wrong and rejoice in the perverseness of evil, whose paths are crooked and who are devious in their ways...THUS YOU WILL WALK IN THE WAYS OF GOOD MEN AND KEEP TO THE PATHS OF THE RIGHTEOUS..."* Pr 2:1-22.

The type of prayer brought forth in Proverbs is an active, intense desire to hear and know God and His ways (call out...cry aloud). As you begin to really know God from His word, His communion with you through prayer, and how He blesses you in your life on earth, you will come to know His nature and ways. He will be speaking to you very personally.

4. God Speaks Through The Human Spirit

God has three basic ways of communicating His will to His children: *1) through visions (a rare event), 2) through a word of knowledge into the mind, and 3) through a consciousness into the spirit.* In true guidance from the Lord, the human mind and spirit are in cooperation sensing with the Holy Spirit what the will of the Lord is and not battling against it from the intellect.

In counterfeit attacks, evil spirits compel a man or woman to act out of fear or "feeling", or from the excitement of a supernatural event. But God does not compel and force man's action. True action flows from the inner harmony of spirit and soul working together to obey the Holy Spirit.

This is why it is so important for believers to know when they are in the spirit or operating from the soul (intellect, will, emotions). The Devil's master scheme is to draw a believer out of his spirit into working from his soul or body, quenching that human spirit from gaining direct God-contact. When that happens, the main task of the human spirit is thwarted from fighting spiritual warfare in prayer, during temptation, and in retaining the power of spirit-detection.

The delicate human spirit that has yet to grow into full strength and richness as the soul and body are put under subjection will falter under attack if it is not heeded. Sometimes you will sense a heaviness or burden or weight. The spirit is not meant to bear these millstones. That is why it is necessary to recognize when you are "down" or being attacked in your spirit. Stop and deal with it by resisting Satan and freeing up your spirit for combat and to direct the personality (Ep 6:13, Ja 4:7) to stand in Christ.

To STAND is a spirit-action of maintaining won ground against any move of the enemy. To WITHSTAND is to boldly defy Satan by godly behavior, the testimony of your mouth, and through prayer. RESISTING the enemy means to actively fight with the spirit much as a man resists by using his fists against another who is physically attacking him. This is the time for righteous anger and was used by Jesus against the money changers who desecrated the temple. He resisted in the physical what was happening in the spiritual.

5. God Speaks Through Correction

Occasionally, everyone finds that he or she has strayed or deliberately stepped off God's Path (His will). In response God's tack is to use love and concern for our welfare by getting the rebellious child (who doesn't want to hear and obey the soft voice) back onto the right Path. Why? because He has a foreordained walk for each child and each child's walk affects the larger plan He works from. It is found in the book of Romans:

"And we know that in ALL things God works for the good of those

who love him, who have been called according to his purpose. For those God foreknew, he also PREDESTINED TO BE CONFORMED TO THE LIKENESS OF HIS SON...If God be for us, who can be against us?" Ro 8:28-31.

"..and you have forgotten that word of encouragement that addresses you as sons: 'My son (My daughter), do not make light of the Lord's discipline, and do not lose heart when he rebukes you because the Lord disciplines those he loves, and he punishes everyone he accepts as a son.' Endure hardship as discipline; God is treating you as sons. For what son is not disciplined by his father? If you are not disciplined (and everyone undergoes discipline), then you are illegitimate children and not true sons. Moreover, we have all had human fathers who disciplined us and we respected them for it.

"How much more should we submit to the Father of our spirits and live! Our fathers disciplined us for a little while as they thought best; BUT God disciplines us FOR OUR GOOD, THAT WE MAY SHARE IN HIS HOLINESS. No discipline seems pleasant at the time, but painful. Later on, however, it produces a harvest of righteousness and peace for those who have been TRAINED by it." Hebrews 12:4-11.

Speaking of correction, God uses many different ways to get our attention so we can proceed along the Path. He may use different grades of harshness in the redirecting process depending on our willingness to submit or the depth of the sin-root involved. Thankfully, we have some control of the process as we choose quickly to hear and obey, or else drag out the disciplining process of God by stubbornness and rebellion.

Do you have a certain problem that seems to set you back and you can't seem to triumph over? To help root it out and bring it to light, God will continually send "odd" circumstances and "pesky" people into your life for you to face that besetting sin once, then face it again and again until you give it up and deal it the death blow. This is a painful move into maturity but once you learn to obey quickly (this is what He is after), you will look back and think how silly and time consuming it was to resist so long and so hard.

Remember when you learned to tie your shoes as a child? You resisted—it was so much easier to let dad, mom, or big sister do it. Then you disciplined yourself to try and try again until mastering it. Afterward, you and your family were so pleased with your new skill. And you never had to relearn tying your shoes. You were then able to move on to more difficult tasks that could build on the lessons learned in shoelace tying.

It is the same in the spirit-life. Your parents' love encouraged and guided you—even though the task ahead was very hard—but you learned and reaped the lifelong benefits. Our Heavenly Father will use all sorts of things to encourage us to move into full stature, just like a gardener. It might only take a little patting of the dirt or several hot, dry days for some; others will need soaking, raking, pruning, or severe cutting down to the root stock.

The point is to obey quickly so you are not treated to some of God's more direct methods of arresting your attention. According to Rev. Charles Stanley of Atlanta, Georgia, some Godly instruments He uses in the maturing process follow:

1. The Word of God tells us plainly what His will is.

2. Family members and friends (those closest to us) can come into hard places, affecting us.

3. Business reversals and financial setbacks—God can withdraw His hand of blessing to remove us from dependance on money or anything at all. When this hindrance is removed, He alone is left — rightfully.

4. The furnace of physical affliction—do you still trust and love God when you are sick, injured, or down? Ask him what the root is so Satan has no victory over you.

5. Trials and Temptations (James 1:2-8)—these instruments are very special and come as a result of standing with Christ; they bring maturity to the mature, and reward in eternity.

"Who (and what) shall separate us from the love of Christ? Shall trouble or hardship or persecution or famine or nakedness or danger or sword? As it is written, 'For your sake we face death all day long; we are considered as sheep to be slaughtered.' NO, in all these things WE ARE MORE THAN CONQUERORS through him who loved us.

"For I am convinced, that neither death, nor life, neither angels nor demons, neither the present nor the future, nor any powers, neither height, nor depth, nor anything else in all creation, will be able to separate us from the love of God that is in Christ Jesus our Lord." Ro 8:35.

To avoid as much corrective discipline and hardship as possible, learn to listen for the voice of God. It is important not to go back to the ways and sins you found yourself in before deliverance. Zealously guard the gifts of God to you.

TO THE EXTENT SOMEONE REQUIRES DELIVERANCE
IS THE EXTENT THEY ARE OFF THE PATH OF GOD.

When you face a temptation no matter how subtle or blatant, remember to listen for the voice of God. Ask some questions: 1) Is this sin?, 2) Will giving in to it hinder my pure walk with God?, 3) Will it bring any kind of harm to me or those I love or seek to win for Christ?, 4) Will I grow stronger or closer to the Lord if I participate in it?, 5) Is it a trap Satan has set to enslave me again?

IMMEDIATELY SUBMIT TO GOD, RESIST THE DEVIL, YOUR OLD NATURE, THE CALL OF THE WORLD, AND PRAISE GOD FOR HIS CARE OVER YOU. DO NOT TAKE EVEN ONE THOUGHT TO GO AFTER WHAT YOU KNOW TO BE WRONG FOR YOU. YOU ALONE ARE RESPONSIBLE TO WALK IN YOUR OWN DELIVERANCE.

SECTION III—The Strength Of Godly Fellowship

Some other useful ways of keeping on God's pathway are found in uniting with others to keep the faith:

1. Commit yourself to a Bible-believing fellowship.
You should not be visiting around or church hopping. Commit to the discipline of the men of God at one fellowship so you come under the protection of the Father. Get to know others for prayer support, fellowship in the Spirit, a place to worship and be free in your new walk. When you need correction, they can help. It is out of this committed relationship and Bible-centered environment that you will be planted and grounded in your faith.

2. Be a Blesssing To Others

You will be feeling very strong as your mind is renewed. A word of caution is not to go looking for a ministry. God is able to raise up a ministry for you where He plants you when He thinks you are ready. A fool rushes out without wise counsel before they are prepared. Ministries built on sand fail every day.

Instead of seeking to be in charge try doing the simple things right before you to bring blessing. The Bible gives this principle: AS you have received, freely give. If you received healing, give healing; if you received forgiveness, forgive others; if you received pardon from your creditors, give pardon to those whom owe you money; if you found the Pearl of great price, give that Pearl to those who need Him. The Lord will specifically open up your gifts to minister to the body. Only an infant RECEIVES all the time. The mature must give, and give again.

> *"Give to EVERYONE WHO ASKS YOU, and if anyone takes what belongs to you, do not demand it back. Do to others as you would have them do to you...Do not judge, and you will not be judged. Do not condemn, and you will not be condemned. Forgive, and you will be forgiven. GIVE, and it will be given to you. A good measure, pressed down, shaken together, and running over, will be poured into your lap. For with the measure you use, it will be measured to you." Lk 6:30-31, 37-38.*

Saint Luke depicts a basic principle of the Kingdom. It works positively for blessing: a believer will receive back everything he or she gives. It also works in the negative: a believer will receive nothing because he or she gave nothing. Seek God for the blessed gift of giving and a big measuring bushel from which to bless the world.

3. Using Your Confession For Freedom

Whenever temptation comes to go a crooked way on the journey in holiness use the CONFESSION OF VICTORY (Appendix I) on a daily basis and whenever needed. You may personalize it with other scriptures the Lord gives as you read the Word. Put your own name in it. This is also a good prayer to use over others because it is simply praying the Word of God. It positions the confessor as standing with God and will prove a great strength in ousting the devil(s) from your presence.

4. Praise the Lord!

Satan hates the Word of God and the praises of God's people. These are two powerful weapons to use on the offense in asserting your legal position before the Lord. Ask God to put a hedge around you, to put His armor on you, and content yourself to be clothed with the fruit of the Holy Spirit (Gal 5:22-26). These actions of your spirit will keep you in step with Him on safe ground.

I sincerely pray you press through on these points. They will take an entire lifetime so don't give in as you learn to be perfected by the Lord. It is a wonderful adventure and supreme challenge because everything human within us fights the whole way. Jesus Christ is calling you to death so you might have abundant Life.

CHAPTER 10

A Word To Intercessory Prayer Counselors

The ministry and calling of an intercessory prayer counselor for deliverance is worthy. Yet it is no more or less special than other specific callings of God. It is a call to death in the servant so that a response to life can be found by those who are helped. Its weapons are glorious yet sharp, unwieldy, and hidden. It is a ministry that is frequently misunderstood even while the cry goes up for renewal in these latter days against the onslaught of the enemy. It demands a person to be worthy of this call.

The Greek word used for worthy as found in the following Bible verses is AXIOS meaning "deserving, comparable, appropriately: as becometh, after a godly sort, worthily; to desire, think good and count meet; to draw praise and due reward." God places a high value on this calling and none dare enter it lightly from self-serving motives. The arena is just too dangerous for that. The Apostle Paul has this admonition:

"..I urge you to LIVE A LIFE WORTHY OF THE CALLING YOU HAVE RECEIVED. Be completely humble and gentle; be patient, bearing with one another in love. Make every effort to keep the unity of the Spirit through the bond of peace. There is one body and one Spirit—just as you were called to one hope when you were called: one Lord, one faith, one baptism; one God and Father of all, who is over all and through all and in all. But to each one of us grace has been give as Christ apportioned it." Ep 4:1-7.

"..that you may LIVE A LIFE WORTHY OF THE LORD and may please him in every way: BEARING FRUIT IN EVERY GOOD WORK, growing in the knowledge of God, being strengthened with ALL POWER according to his glorious might so that you may have great endurance and patience, and joyfully giving thanks *to the Father, who has qualified you to share in the inheritance of the saints in the kingdom of light. For he has rescued us from the dominion of darkness and brought us into the kingdom of the Son he loves, in whom we have redemption (deliverance), the forgiveness of sins."* Col 1:10-14.

"You are witnesses, and so is God, of how HOLY, RIGHTEOUS AND BLAMELESS we were among you who believed. For you know that we dealt with each of you as a father deals with his own children, ENCOURAGING, COMFORTING, AND URGING YOU TO LIVE LIVES WORTHY OF GOD, who calls you into his kingdom and glory." 1 Th 2:10-12.

Some Qualifications Of This Ministry

We cannot know all the qualifications and graces God bestows and grows in his servants for this type of ministry. While an admittedly incomplete list is included here, the basic considerations from the author's experience are presented. In all cases, the prayer counselor should be under the direct authority of a pastor or priest and in constant contact with him regarding what the Lord is doing and how He is leading. Having a spiritual director will provide the balance needed in the ministry and prevent a great deal of wasted effort and treading on dangerous ground.

Intercessory prayer for deliverance is not an independent, maverick ministry that is done over afternoon crumpets and tea. It is a serious calling with an annointing (Is 61:1), carried out under the authority of the spiritual headship of Jesus Christ. Prayer counselors who are moving in the walk of faith with spiritual gifts manifested, are:

1. You have personally experienced salvation.
2. You have followed the Lord in water baptism.
3. You have received the Baptism of the Holy Spirit and are ALREADY functioning in your gifts of the Spirit.
4. You have established a relationship with God whereby you hear His voice, obey it, and are an example to others.
5. You are walking with the Lord in no known or unconfessed sin and are open to the ministry of others regarding sin in your own life.
6. You have a submissive, servant spirit, and the annointing of God for this ministry.
7. You are in the Word and prayer in a disciplined way.

8. You are willing to submit yourself for deliverance before beginning this ministry and at any time necessary in order to remain a clean vessel.

9. You are recognized by your pastor/priest and your fellowship as a servant worthy of this calling.

10. You have come under training and are prepared for the ministry of intercessory prayer for deliverance.

Ministering Deliverance In Love

Ideally, this ministry comes out of a church body set up for deliverance that can process the requests as they arise. There is an orderly way of handling counselling opportunities so that prayer ministers are not rushed (usually by the counselee) or too hasty to minister before all is in place. Be assured that nothing will happen to the counselee while those in charge are finding the will of God for the appropriate counselor team, the place to minister, or for any spiritual preparations needed before and during ministry. Satan and the flesh compels and propels: the Holy Spirit however, is gentle and timely, never pushy.

In helping to form teams for the ministry there are some basic common sense considerations. For instance, intercessory prayer counsellors (like all Christians) are to avoid all appearances of evil. For this reason and for self-protection that Satan has no place to trip you, counsellors should be paired in groups of two or at the most three.

As a rule of thumb it is advisable to use any combination of males and females on a team of three. Two women as a unit or two men together on a duel team is fine. A husband and wife team can prove very strong in this ministry and is especially beneficial in post-deliverance counselling for families.

Usually a special room is set aside at the church where deliverance can take place in a controlled area that can be spiritually sealed. These rooms can be equipped with proper chairs, privacy (no telephone), a small restroom facility if possible, tissues for tears, etc. It is a neutral room that may be scheduled for specific prayer use and will not contain familiar objects or distractions. Having it in the church brings the blessing of the pastor and congregation by making it a body ministry.

Or, deliverance may be accomplished in a home setting that can provide the same privacy. I have assisted in room deliverance (about 20 people) where people came forward one by one to sit in a chair directly in front of the prayer counselor for personal ministry. It is highly effective after intense teaching has taken place. This does not prove to be the best place for deep ministry and must be done in a trusting communal atmosphere.

Before beginning any session it is good to explain that at times the prayer counselors may sound angry, commanding, demanding or intense. Remember that the counselee is a PERSON with feelings, needs, perceptions, a capacity for communication, and is quite vulnerable at this point of need. YOU are the one who is mature, has understanding, and is walking with the Lord in holiness. It is up to you to present the Lord Jesus Christ and not your own personality or personal traits during these sessions.

While it is true that prayer counselors are directly communicating in the spiritual, the counselee is listening to every word and should be cautioned that team members are not speaking with them but against the forces of darkness in them. Communicate this clearly so they understand that warfare is a personal attack against Satan and not against them. The Holy Spirit in you is fighting the demonic while they "listen in".

Be cautioned not to be side tracked by the revelation of some sin by thinking or speaking out an immediate answer to "solve the problem". This is not called for. Actual deliverance is not the place to reform or train counsellees with problems. Rather remain concentrated on the war against Satan on their behalf. It is like a competitive game of chess: you can play around on the board, or you can steadily move in to capture the king piece and win.

Intercessory prayer for deliverance is a totally confidential ministry. There is no need or scriptural basis for a counselor to share anything with anyone of what was seen or heard during the time of ministry. If "well-meaning" people ask for particulars, firmly admonish them not to ask. A simple, "I'm sorry, that's between them and the Lord", should do it. You value the counselee and would not purposely handicap him or her in their efforts to leave the past behind them. Be very strict about this. Once deliverance is a part of the fellowship and you remain hidden in the ministry, these situations will not arise.

Spiritual warfare can be highly exhilarating at times as victory after victory is won. Counselors must be careful to realize that whatever great breakthroughs happen belong to the counselee's testimony—not to yours. Personal testimony comes from wanting to share what God is doing with and in them. They may choose to never share. Respect their privacy and realize that the prayer counselor is but a hidden servant of God, His vessel that the water of the Word passes through on its way to healing. It is amazing to realize that you will not remember much of what happens anyway. Leave it to the Lord.

Experience and maturity in the use of this ministry will serve to precaution those called to never seek "demons under every bush". They are not there. God will give you ministry through your pastor who is in a position to see what the Lord is doing in the whole church or in agreement with other team members. But people who seek demonic encounters as a warrior of the Lord without being in order and protected will find themselves open to deception and ministering out of season. This self-serving behavior will only bring discouragement and take the power of God from you. Rather, wait on the Lord. You will be used as He sees fit. This is part of being a humble and submissive servant, one sensitive to God's timing and love.

The Ministry Is A Body Outreach

The deliverance ministry is one of the local church when allowed. It is an extension of Christ to the community and the whole body of believers should be aware of it not only for themselves but as people come to them in need. There is a great desire that many individual and varied church members involve themselves in the ministry by serving as back-up prayer warriors before and during deliverance, as schedulers, with room preparation and clean-up, in post-deliverance counselling, and fellowship follow-up.

After deliverance, it is nice for a team member to personally introduce the counselee to those in the fellowship who have other gifts like helps, giving, teaching, prophesy, and encouragement. Deliverance is but a beginning point of a person's new or renewed walk with the Lord. Involve them with others to speed the healing process and provide the role models for keeping their deliverance fresh and vibrant.

> "To every thing there is a season and a time to every purpose under the heaven..a time to love, and a time to hate; a TIME OF WAR, and a time of peace." Ec 3:1,8 (KJV).

The Discerning of Spirits

The gift of discernment of spirits (1 Co 12:10) speaks on three levels when it is in operation because some demons like to manifest themselves and will especially do so, when they are stirred up. The Name of Jesus Christ is a powerful stir-tool.

Chapter 10

1. Manifesting in the Body

Sight: In the natural physical world, we are able to see, hear, smell, sense, and touch (skin sensation) the effects of the operations of spirits (possible with both good and evil spirits). With evil spirits their effect on a person is seen through coughing, spitting, choking, writhing, blinking, yawning, crying, and the like. They also take other forms which may be seen (Re 16:13; Ge 18:1-2; Lk 24:36-37). Evil spirits can indwell inanimate "familiar" objects decorated with zodiacal symbols, voodoo masks, Gautama Buddhas, idols, etc.

Hearing: It is possible to hear the spirits use the vocal cords of people when they cause them to cry, shout, shriek, laugh, mock, speak, groan, mutter, growl, whisper or call out (Lk 8:28-30; Mk 1:23-24; Ac 19:15; 2 Ki 7:6). I have heard them sing vulgar show tunes with striptease music and project a masculine voice from a woman's vocal cords. A frightened demon (self-pity, fear, shyness) may whimper, cloud up the counselee's eyes with tears and pitifully beg to stay behind. Do not tolerate that for a moment but cast them out.

Touch: There are more instances of God's Spirit touching humans than evil spirits touching humans; however, it is possible to touch a person's skin and find it cold and clammy, especially the extremities where evil spirits linger. Counselees may complain of feeling "spooky", cold or blown upon (Ju 6:21; 1 Ki 19:5-7).

Some counselees have testimonies of having been beaten, raped, or spat upon but these demonic antics are never tolerated during counseling sessions because they don't get that far. Praise God, the Name of Jesus stops physical abuse or tearing by spirits during deliverance should it occur at all.

Smell: 2 Co 2:14-16 speaks of the aroma of Christ as a sweet-smelling fragrance, the opposite of the odor of death which is putrid, fetid, rancid, vile, and raises a stench. Certain demons (drugs, is one) emit a terrible smell with bad breath, in vomiting or through the skin. I have seen pale smoke come out of a counselee's nose when the spirit of tobacco was cast out.

Whole Body Sense: Job 4:5 *"A spirit glided past my face, and the hair on my body stood on end."* Counselees may feel spirits leave by their

130

hands (e.g., arthritis, cancer) or through their feet and toes (dirty dancing, mischief, ground demons), crossing their skin as they exit. This is a common occurrence in deliverance and when confronting any of these manifestations command that spirit(s) to go in Jesus' Name without bodily attack or delay.

2. Manifesting in the Mind

Spirits may manifest themselves in dreams or visions, nightmares and trances. Familiar spirits will sometimes make themselves known at seances (Mt 1:20; 2:12-19; Ge 31:11). This is often where counselees began to have supernatural revelations of the spirit world. Hearing Satan or his demons speak is common because he loves to tell lies into people's minds. Some people will see them and report on them during deliverance.

Primarily, all manner of Satan-implanted temptation comes to the mind first. It may or may not move into the natural senses as it is either given into or resisted. For instance, the seed of all sin begins by thinking on it. This stage may take years or just moments when the contemplation to sin goes into blossom by acting on the suggestion. Temptation turns to sin by decision. However, Satan does not make a person sin. He cleverly uses his wiles (methods) to weaken and expose us to acts contrary to God's will (Ro 1:20-32) whereby a choice to sin is set up.

Surprisingly, it is not always the wicked devils who try to first gain entrance to the errant Christian or worldly-wise. They can be bidden to reside when one opens himself or herself up to their spheres of work. Ripe mind-sets (Chapter 3) beg evil spirits to make contact with anyone seeking "spiritual enlightenment", and is especially true of occultic experiences.

Deceiving spirits appeal to the soul and often put in their appearance in humanistic, pseudo-medical, or psychological self-help sessions led by spiritists in which clients are encouraged (and sometimes taught how) to contact their "spirit guide", to hear voices, or get visions. Recently at one of the annual international witches conferences, seminars were held for witches on "Learning Angelic Languages". This is a counterfeit of God's gift of speaking in tongues and serves to entrap witches (who desperately need Christ) still deeper in Satanic mire.

When counselees tell the team what the demon is saying or will speak out its words in the deliverance session, prayer counselors should deal with these evil forces harshly and tell them to be silent. It is suggested that you ask the Holy Spirit to reveal and expose them like this:

"Holy Spirit in John, who is this demon speaking?" Or, "Who is John seeing now?" The counselee will answer back from his or her spirit.

Then say, "Foul spirit of _____ (whatever was named), I bind you in the Name of Jesus Christ." "John, is the demon bound?" He will answer from his human spirit what he sees. Deal with it until the demon is bound.

When this is done, tell the counselee to reject and cast out of himself the spirit of_____ in the Name of Jesus Christ. They must be very forceful at this point because this breaks the legal rights of the demonic to stay.

DO NOT GIVE TIME TO LISTENING TO DEMONS OR ASKING THEIR NAMES. MOVE THEM OUT OF THERE IN FAITH. THEY LOVE TO DELAY THEIR DEPARTURE, HINDER, AND WASTE TIME.

Some questions which are useful are, "Holy Spirit in (person's name), please tell him what the legal right is that has allowed Satan to remain?" Or, "Holy Spirit, please tell us if there are any other open doors that remain in John." "What are they?"

Another question might be, "Holy Spirit, is John free of all demonic influences in his body?" Get an answer. Then leave deliverance or pursue the enemy further. And, "Is John free in his soul?" "Holy Spirit, is John free in his spirit?"

Any demon who has cursed a person can have that same curse brought down on them. "You foul demon who caused the curse of witchcraft in this family, may it be visited upon you now in the Name of Jesus Christ. The curse of God comes against you now. You go out of John now, and go to your punishment. You go. Go tell your master how you failed him."

Here is your spiritual weapons permit: Psalm 149:5-9, 2 Corinthians 10:6, and Matthew 12:29. The Psalms are liberally sprinkled with warfare passages.

Dealing With "Stop-Stills" In Deliverance Sessions

A word must be said regarding the occasional occurrence of a counselee who refuses to give up, renounce, or repent of some sin. What does the counselor do then? First you must be sure you are speaking to the counselee and not to any demon. When you address the counselee by his (or her) name you will get an answer from them. If you are unsure it is indeed him, demand in the Name of Jesus that he look into your eyes and answer you until you are sure you are speaking with him. Then ask him to cooperate by repenting and renouncing that particular spirit who refuses to go.

Normally the counselee desires to be rid of all evil entities. They were the ones who initiated action from the church or counselor by requesting help. Pre-session questioning should have revealed what they perceived as basic difficulties. However, if in the course of deliverance there is a refusal to repent or renounce sin in one specific area (e.g., homosexuality) the deliverance session must stop. Do not work further in that or any area. Withholding forgiveness is another stopper. Gently close down to that rebellion and unbelief that holds back their own healing.

Prayer counselors can create stop-stills. Be on guard that deliverance is not rushed into without observing the preliminary steps outlined. Prayer counselors who are disobedient to God's voice when a word of knowledge is given, or who do not bind the spirits in the person or fail to spiritually seal the room (against other demons "coming to their comrades' rescue") leaves outside doors open to continue the session beyond necessity.

Another way to encounter a solid wall is when counselors themselves are not clean vessels thereby lending support and reinforcement to unclean spirits in the counselee. Preparatory intercession for the counselee must be given and the prayer team must work in unity. Jesus Himself stated that a period of prayer and fasting is sometimes needed to cast them out.

When there is an obvious stop-still, relate this to the one you are praying for and be sensitive in closing the session. Bind all spirits from harming him or her until future arrangements can be made to continue. More teaching and counseling is needed and they should be scheduled to receive it from those so gifted.

One particular stop-still came when we were praying with a woman who went through the whole deliverance process until we came to suicide. Right there she stated that she had nothing to live for and adamantly expressed her plans to take pills and starve herself to death to "teach her exhusband a lesson". She would not repent of these death wishes! It was obvious she needed intensive counseling and teaching given by a spiritual director. Since deliverance was not the place for either of these we closed the session over her protests. She later made a renewed commitment to Christ and was lovingly helped through some rough spots by the body of Christ over a period of time before deliverance was again REQUESTED BY HER and given with success.

You may encounter the death spirit. In people with this, there is a deep, internal conviction—especially in death and life choices—that is made to either embrace life or embrace death. Those who want life show it by taking care of their bodies, putting on seat belts, watching their weight and what they ingest, and by immersing themselves in positive, healthy activities and friendships. People who choose life, choose to fight inertia, early death, all manner of illness from the common cold to raging cancers and will seek God's help and deliverance when they sense danger or overwhelming circumstance.

People who embrace death will resign themselves when confronted with a deadly cancer diagnosis. They view it as a "noble way to go" or a good reason to just give up on living. Often they fulfill their physician's time frame by dying right on schedule ("You've got six months to live"). Other internal choices for death over life are seen in continuing a stress-filled lifestyle, seeking "death-defying" adventures, adopting and continuing addictive and negative habits, or passively giving in to depression or the deliberate prolonging of illness.

Be aware that Satan's method is to kill all the children of promise. His purpose is not to maim BUT TO KILL and deliver us surely into his pits. The righteous pious Christian must never give up life because of "incurable" illnesses, the onset of old age, or intolerable living conditions. We must be absolutely positive our lifework is over and God is calling us home before we say yes to God.

Our example·is Jesus Christ. Did Calvary's cross kill Jesus? No, absolutely not! He gave His spirit back to God when He said "Into Your hands I commend my spirit" Why? because He knew His human lifework had been completed (Lk 23:46; Jn 19:29-30; Mt 27:50). Yes, His whole purpose in coming to earth was to die for humankind's sin: but not until He determined by the counsel of His Father the exact second. And He did not hand His spirit to Satan, He gently handed it to His Father.

Rest A While . . .

It is probable during very heavy deliverance to get only so far when the counselee will need to rest and take time to digest what has happened to him or her. Time to walk out the deliverance already received strengthens new insights received during the session. Resting between times should include Bible study. Deliverance is a ministry that prayer counselors do not "do" to someone, but with them because counselees must be 100% involved and committed to ridding themselves of demonic spirits.

Without a doubt, God will give counselors a word of wisdom during a session (ask Him) as to why it may be time to stop or perhaps why a particular demon won't come out right then. It is up to the counselor to be sensitive to what the Lord is doing and humbly obey. This is love. And love does not rush God's process.

> *"And he said unto them, 'This kind can come forth by nothing, but prayer and fasting.' "* Mk 9:29, Mt 17:21 (KJV).

> *"Is not this the FAST that I have chosen? To loose the bands of wickedness, to undo the heavy burdens, and to let the oppressed go free, and that ye break every yoke?"* Is 58:6 (KJV).

> *"Be careful for nothing; but in everything by prayer and supplication with thanksgiving let your requests be made known unto God."* Phil 4:6 (KJV).

> *"As for me, I will call upon God; and the Lord shall save me. Evening, and morning, and at noon, will I pray, and cry aloud: and He shall hear my voice. He hath delivered my soul in peace from the battle that was against me: for there were many with me."* Ps 55:16-18 (KJV).

What Are Some Common Demon Families?

Demons are as powerful in acting within a person as believed to be. What I mean by that is that demons are quite weak and helpless when confronted with the Word of God, with the worship of God, and with the power of the Name and Blood of Jesus. These wicked little guys will turn tail and run when exposed and expelled. Deliverance is nothing like what the sensational and worldly-popular movies present. Why? because God's children are protected by His blood and Satan is not God: is not omnipresent, omniscient, nor omnificent.

When left to develop on their own in a backslidden life, demons seem to find strength in clutches of families. Many come into the person together and need to go out together. There is often a strongman or strongmen who hold the families together and will sacrifice the weaker demons (when confronted) in order to maintain their own territory, position, and power.

Evil spirits have differing levels of "strength" because they have either been allowed full rein in a life, have been coddled (i.e., self-pity), or their presence is used for personal power by the possessed person. Strength and confidence of remaining in the "family" builds as one continues to walk in besetting sins (i.e., willful addictive habits).

The opposite is also true. Spirits can come out quite easily during times of worship and praise given by overcoming Christians because sin has never been allowed to root itself into the spirit, soul, or body. Some deliverance can be as mild as a yawn in one believer while she or he is praying deliverance for another.

> *"Dear friends, do not believe every spirit, but TEST THE SPIRITS to see whether they are from God, because many false prophets have gone out into the world. This is how you can recognize the Spirit of God: Every spirit that acknowledges that Jesus Christ has come in the flesh is from God, but every spirit that does not acknowledge Jesus, is not from God. This is the spirit of the antichrist, which you have heard is coming and EVEN NOW IS ALREADY IN THE WORLD. You, dear children, are from God and have overcome them, BECAUSE THE ONE WHO IS IN YOU IS GREATER THAN THE ONE WHO IS IN THE WORLD."* 1 Jn 4:1-3.

For the following family groupings, I have endeavored to point out the strongman/men by naming their families. From experience, demon families tend to change around and abide with those whom they are most comfortable and least likely to be discovered with and booted out. You will in actual ministry, no doubt, come across different groupings with different strongmen. This listing is only given for informational purposes and is strickly subject to the Holy Spirit in you!

Demons have different names in other cultures and I have found from sessions in South America that even without knowing the local language, spirits can be expelled in your own language without the understanding of the counselee because spirits know all languages—heavenly and human. The gift of Diversities of Tongues is very helpful here, causing great consternation in the demonic realms. The Name and Blood of Jesus Christ is very powerful in all languages—praise God!

Be Specific in Your Spiritual Understanding

A word of explanation is in order before reading the various demon families. Be very careful to understand what some of the names on these lists mean. Because some acts or attitudes are named here does not necessarily mean they are sinful or demonic. Take the example of "debate". In the case of one having an overpowering love of debate (aggressive argumentativeness) serving as a possessing force within them, it is enslavement and must be released. To another Christian debate may be a practical way to air opinion or take a scriptural stand in a secular situation like a classroom. That debate is not sinful nor demonic.

Each area should be prayfully questioned. The counselee will bear witness to Truth in their spirits whenever the Word of Knowledge goes forth putting a finger on a besetting sin. It is helpful for counselors to be familiar with the various families to try the spirits for ridding the whole nest at once.

In all cases, the Holy Spirit is your guide and will reveal Himself by His gifts to the praying team. It is also possible that several sessions will be needed by a person over a period of months or years—as he or she is ready to relinquish control and allow God access.

1. THE FAMILY OF FEAR

All common fears: fear of reproof, intrepidation, the fears of animals, germs, people, heights, loneliness, spiders, darkness, death, future, failure, rejection, suffering, pain, the unknown, being robbed, accusations, disapproval, judgment, condemnation, religious figures, public places, small places, blindness, sex, intimacy, poverty, wealth, snakes, demons, madness, and all kinds of fears—whatever a demon can convince a person to be afraid of.

Other members in this family may be: insecurity, doubting, unbelief, fear of fears, nervousness, pills, shyness, timidity, anger, passivity, allergies, mind control, clumsiness, sickness, blank mind, and the spirit of unemployment or poverty.

2. THE FAMILY OF LIARS

Lying, perjury, deceit, deception, pretense, exaggeration, pride, falsehood, play-acting the truth, false accusations, hypocrisy, wee liar, cute lies, white lies, black lies, cunning, affectation, fakery, con-man, unreality, insincerity, sophistication, double-crossing, indian-giver, daydreaming, fantasy, theatrics, jaunty, aggrandizement, changed my mind, unfaithfulness, transvestite, homosexual, confusion, selfishness, broken vows, crime, thief, sarcasm, cynicism, hopelessness, unbelief, adultery, slander, gossip, independent spirit.

There is an "Ananias spirit" which promises God something then with-holds it, and a "Sapphira spirit" which is one person covering (lying as an accessory to) another's sin (Acts 5).

3. THE FAMILY OF PRIDE

Pride, I am god, man-divine, vanity, ego, covetousness, greed, ar-rogance, boastfulness, conceit, anorexia, bulimia, pride of life, haughti-ness, false pride, spiritual pride, pride of competition, vain glory, snootiness, snobbishness, uppity spirit, elitism, indignation, mockery, su-periority, inferiority, extravagance, waste, indulgence, miserliness (false pride), fame, pride of intellectualism, religious pride ("My denomination is..).

Leviathan (king of the children of pride-Job 41:1), top dog, top gun, spiritual eyes blinded, closed spirit, domination, possessiveness, materi-alism, enlightener, Jezebel spirit, intolerance, loudness to dominate, body-fixation, fear, divorce, rejection, physical or verbal abuse ("I am stronger"), materialism (I own the most/best), perfectionism (all or noth-ing thinking), narcissism, mutilation, a Diotrephes spirit ("I am in charge").

4. THE FAMILY OF BONDAGE

Cravings for addictive substances such as marijuana, heroin, all illegal drugs, wild herbs and mushrooms that are hallucigenic, prescription drugs that are security-addictive, liquors, wines, alcohol, caffeine in colas, chocolate, medicine, tea, coffee, foods, sugar, glue sniffing, and any halu-cigens made or found in nature that appeals to the flesh.

Compatible members in bondage could include Legion, gluttony, in-temperance, hypodermic needles, the DTs, self-indulgence, slavery, bondage to religion, racism, KKK, Female's militant movement, gay rights movement, compulsiveness, Occult activities, sacrifice, mar-tyrdom, male or female dominance, lies, rock music, magic, ethnic roots that control families; television, subliminal suggestion, hypnosis, trance, visualization, gambling, lotto, lottery, bingo, all games of chance, precog-nition, ESP, bad habits, hand-writing analysis; ouija, spirit of poverty, an-cestor worship and national or social bonds.

5. THE FAMILY OF REBELLION

Hostility, malice, hatred, temper, strife, rage, anger, envy, jealousy, mischievousness, spite, disputing, misunderstanding, backbiting, bitterness, argument, aggression, competitiveness, unreasonableness, despising, error, misconduct, derision, opposition, division, vengeance, sadism, quarreling, lust, unforgiveness, retaliation, cruelty, meanness, bully, impudence, contention, disobedience, bickering, frustration, slander, arson, crime against nature, vindictiveness, inhospitality, anti-golden rule, agitation, nervousness, harshness, disloyalty, treason, insubordination, and uncivility.

Others include enmity, murder, abortion, suicide, infanticide, genocide, animal murder (killing, but not for food or control), bribery, torture, hurtful, slander, gossip, selfishness, defile the environment, hippy, nonconformity, blasphemy, belittling, railing, accusation, pitilessness, stoic, tense, indifference, silence as punishment, hedonism, froward mouth, defiant attitude, independance, unbelief, trouble-maker, gangs, cults, I will, love-killer, Communism, Nazism, traitor, dictator, tyrant, evil discrimination, polygamy, Absalom spirit.

6. THE FAMILY OF THE PSYCHE

These attack the soul with schizophrenia, multi-personality, double-mindedness, mental disorders, illness, psychology, vain imaginations, seared conscience, mania, mental weakness, madness, crazy, insanity, derangement, anxiety, intellectualism, doubt, unbelief, paranoia, retardation, indiscrimination, imbecility, senility, hallucinations, tension, worry, frustration, division, incoherence, forgetfulness, nervousness, headache, migraine, dread, nervous habits, restlessness, insomnia, apprehension, stress, gloom, depression, despair, despondency, discouragement, defeatism, dejection, complaints, power, and death.

Others include hopelessness, disgust, suicide, morbidity, burden, heaviness, barking, uncanny laughter, skepticism, mind roving, dissatisfaction, control by dreams, cowardice, rashness, glum, improvidence, twitching, fidgeting, misery, ignorance, hesitation, pessimism, instability, despondence, melancholy, mournful, neglectfulness, loss of memory, faltering, faint-heartedness, wavering, overbearing competitiveness, driving spirits, heartache, rationalization, pressure, grief, sorrow, sadness, fatigue, talkativeness, mind control; sectarianism and false religion, cults, fear, irrationality, panic, debate and Legion.

7. THE FAMILY OF PERVERSION

Lust, vice, lust of the eye, illicit sexual desire, perversity, filthiness, unclean, abusive, passion, ravishment, sex against animals, wild affections, anal sex, forced sex, impurity, fornication, rape, adultery, lasciviousness, root of sexual impurity, carnality, dirty dancing, incest (Moab spirit), harlotry, idolatry, provocativeness, filthy thoughts, sodomy, whoredoms, prostitution, child molestation, seduction, foulness, vulgarity, defilement, filthy conversation and unclean jokes or jesting, sexual indulgence, homosexuality, lesbianism, immorality, fantasy lust, all pornography, sexual fantasy, genital exposure, flashing, frigidity, impotence, unfaithfulness, unholiness, falatio, cunnilingus, degradation, debasement, deprivation, and bestiality.

Others are: Love gods/goddesses, Baal, Astarte, Ashtoreth, fertility worship, depravity, inordinate affection for animals, phalic or sexual symbols, nudity, immodesty, Legion, sadism, masochism, sadomasochism, fear of sex, hatred of sex, retrobate, compulsive, tempter, flirt, root of perversion, enticement, Venus, Eros, fetish, torture, unusual crimes against nature, liar, obscenity, playboy, gigolo, stud, playgirl-sexual mistress, VD (all veneral diseases).

8. THE FAMILY OF INFIRMITIES

Blind, deaf and dumb spirits; convulsion, cancers, fevers, allergies and pride of allergies, tumor, epilepsy, narcolepsy, pain, weakness, sickness, infirmity, infection, bronchitis, swelling, cold, pleurisy, heart trouble, death, pneumonia, virus, diabetes, asthma, arthritis, AIDS and pre-AIDS.

Others can come in like senility, crippling, self-pity, worry, attention-getter, manipulation, immaturity, fetus worship, fetus murder, idolatry, rebellion, unbelief, death wish, arthritis (often comes with critical spirit), hate, suicide, euthanasia, female (reproductive) sicknesses or impotency, and "family" diseases.

9. THE FAMILY OF RELIGIOUS SPIRITS

Witchcraft, spirit of Baal, Molech, spiritualist, fortune telling, ouija board, psychic readings, voodoo, tea leaf, cranium reading, numerology, medium, familiar spirits, enchantment, wizard, hypnotism, palm reading, table tilting, crystal ball, anything occult, crystals, water witching warlock, handwriting analysis, automatic writing, horoscope, astrology, pendulum, black and white magic, charms, conjuration, incantation, Mary-Mother of God worship, fetishes, religiousness, ritualism, formalism, legalism, necromancy, false religion, ALL cults (Islam, Moonies, Hari Krishna, Jehovah's Witness, Christian Science, Urantia, Rosicrucianism, Theosophy, Subudd, Unity, Mormonism, Bahaism, Unitarianism, Buddhism, Tao, Hinduism, New Age, One World Unity, Communism, Nazism, KKK, Atheism, Agnosticism, etc.).

Religious spirits come in with the Book of Mormon, Satanic or New Age bibles, dominion theology, devilish piety, anti-christian activity, worldliness, Satan's kingdom, idolatry, false sacrifice, blind obedience, willful disobedience, penance, apostasy, heresy, delusion, misinterpretation, false burden, persecution, seance, spirit guides, false compassion, false ministry, darkness, clairvoyant, jezebel, worship of religious figures (living or dead) or religious icons and idols, Aseamta, Eckankar (soul travel) Pharisaism, Sadducism, error, Tarot, Faro, bondage, metaphysics, death and hell worship.

Other entry doors include: imaginary friends, doctor worship, Goddess Rah, Mark of the Beast, religious symbols (Inverted Pentagram, 666, Upside-down cross, broken cross, peace symbol, the hex, unicorn, all-seeing eye, occultic and celestial symbols, satanic-worship symbols), rascism, False Prophet, false religion, false teachers, false apostles, UFO fixation, Philistine spirit, clergy-worship, and an Alexander spirit (undermines spiritual leadership).

10. THE FAMILY OF SELF-CENTEREDNESS

These hyphenated words each begin with "self" and show the direction of centering in the soul area: self-pity, self-will, self-consciousness, self-conceit, self-righteousness, self-content, self-sufficiency, self-justification, self-deception, self-rejection, self-delusion, self-seduction, self-hatred, self-centeredness, self-condemnation, self-indulgence self-adoration, and self-protector. This list can be almost endless because it depends on the priority and idolatry in a life.

All selfishnesses: any emotion or trait that centers on or around the self-life, guilt(s), hypocrisy, inferiority, shame, slackness, false security, superiority, false peace, grumbling, complaining, fault-finding, neglect, judging, criticism, no self-worth, suspicion, distrust, martyrdom, passivity, escapism, fantasy, withdrawal, stoicism, lethargy, slumbering spirit, inaction, possessiveness, control, shyness, jealousy, and a hasty spirit (me too, me first, me only).

11. THE FAMILY OF WORLDLINESS

Love of the world, foolishness, inconsistency, laziness, greed, competition, success, love of money, habitual welfare support from anywhere, cowardice, insufficiency, wrong diligence, pickpocket, unfruitfulness, curse of God, ungodliness, career god, unscrupulousness, indolence, dishonesty, pouting, dishonor, vacillation, taking advantage, prosperity idol, "I deserve" spirit, impulsiveness, envy, jealousy, covetousness.

Worldliness can come in with procrastination, perfectionism, critical spirit, comparing with man, lust for business, clothes horse, trend-setter, love of vehicles (obsession), vain philosophies, over-education, pride, murder of reputation, bankruptcy, frivolous legal suits, warmonger, merciless, cheat, superficial, know-it-all, mockery, show-off, worldly-wise, serpent, pride, vain ambition, party spirit, haughty, commercialism, politicking for spiritual favor, wastefulness and decadent lifestyle.

12. THE FAMILY OF PRINCIPALITIES

Islam, Vashti, Jezebel, Herod, Babylon, Leviathan, Behemoth, Apollyon, Chongo, Gog/Magog, Sodom-Gomorrha, Laban, Jubal, Haman, Anti-Christ, Anti-semitism, Pride, Satanas, Caesars, Death, Hell, Greek gods (Apollos, Mars, Jupiter, Saturn, Pluto, Hermes, etc.), Chaos, Cush, Molek, Moab, Beelzebub, Lord of the Flies, Dagon, The Beast, Powers of the Air, False Prophet, and Anti-Christ.

There are particular demons over families, cities, nations, and continents; the Spirit of Devils (Re 16:14), Legion, Baal, Ashtoreth, the Red Dragon (Re 12), Angel of Light, and the Rulers, Authorities and Powers of the dark or netherworld (Ep 6:12).

This is not an exhaustive list of principalities and powers. Prayer warrior-intercessors have stood for their cities and nations to uncover all principalities having power and authority over their geographic areas because the Lord reveals it to them.

Just to Encourage You...

As prayer counselors, may I please ask you to search your spirits to be sure within that the Lord is the center of the intentions of your heart in this ministry. Pray about looking for opportunities for ministry to stand in the gap and help to set up a ministry in your fellowship. Success will be what God determines it to be and you may be called to be a part of that success.

Please read the Appendices which are rich in deeper understanding of just what the Spirit of God in you is fighting against to free His children. Consider providing, with the permission of your spiritual head, a copy of this manual to be read by all counselees before your team attempts ministry. I believe it will save much teaching time for you and ready them to receive from the Lord in the specific areas needing that Divine touch of the Master.

As your sister in Christ I would personally appreciate your writing to me with your experiences, reactions, and victories at the address given in the front of this book at Word Vision Ministries. May our Father God love, guide, and keep you strong as you work and serve in His kingdom.

APPENDIX

APPENDIX I — The Confession of Victory

The Confession of Victory is compiled of scriptures that can and will renew your mind and assist in conforming you to the image of Jesus Christ. There is power in the confession of the mouth that goes into the human spirit, out to the Heavenly Father, and to where all principalities and powers can hear and realize that the confessor means commitment to Almighty God.

As a preliminary to deliverance, the prayer team and counselee may read this together as an affirmation of their spiritual position. It is best READ ALOUD WITH CONVICTION.

As post-deliverance follow-up, the counselee will find this confession very strengthening in the morning or at any time of stress or attack. There is no "magical" quality about the confession. It is not a substitute for prayer or Bible reading. Think of it as an aid to centering on the Word of God to remember all His promises to you as His child.

THE CONFESSION OF VICTORY

HOLY, HOLY, HOLY IS THE LORD GOD ALMIGHTY: WHO WAS, AND IS, AND IS TO COME. [1]

You are worthy, our Lord and God, to receive glory and honor and power for you created all things, and by your will they were created and have their being. [2]

Worthy is the Lamb who was slain to receive power and wealth and wisdom and strength and honor and glory and praise! [3]

I CONFESS and believe that Jesus is the Christ and that I am born of God. I love you God, my Father, and want to obey and carry out Your commands. This, my faith, has overcome the world. [4]

My righteousness comes from God through my faith in the blood of Jesus Christ. [5]

Therefore, I no longer have any condemnation or guilt because I am in Christ Jesus and the Spirit of Life has set me free from the law of sin and death. [6]

I have the Word of God in me because I have confessed my sins and have been purified from all unrighteousness. [7]

I came to Jesus because the Father enabled me to come and now I speak the Words of Life because they are the Words of Christ which are Spirit and Life. [8]

I have taken off my old self with its practices and have put on the new self which is being renewed in knowledge to the image of its Creator. Therefore, I am a new person: holy, dearly loved, clothed with compassion, kindness, humility, gentleness and patience. I have the Peace of Christ ruling in my heart. [9]

Jesus Christ came by water and by blood and His Spirit testifies to this truth, for these three are in agreement and I testify that I have eternal life because Life is in the Son and I have the Son. [10]

I have followed Christ in water baptism according to His example and have been baptized in the Holy Spirit. [11]

I came to Jesus Christ because I was thirsty and I drank. Since I have believed in Him as the scripture has said, streams of living water flow from within me. [12]

I have received the baptism of the Holy Spirit with fire and am complete. [13]

I accept and believe that You, O Lord, will fulfill Your purpose for me; that Your love endures forever…for You have searched and known me even when I sit and when I rise. You God, perceive my thoughts and are familiar with all my ways. You hem me in from behind and before and have laid Your hand of blessing on me. [14]

Now the Spirit witnesses with my spirit that I am His child, heir, and joint-heir with Christ because I do share in His sufferings. [15]

I can do everything through Him who gives me strength. [16]

I claim to be filled by God with the knowledge of His will through the engifting of spiritual wisdom and understanding. [17]

I do, right now, offer my body as a living sacrifice to God which is holy and pleasing to Him. It is my spiritual act of worship. I choose not to be conformed to the pattern of the world but to be transformed by the renewing of my mind. [18]

Now my God has rescued me from the dominion of darkness and brought me into the kingdom of the Son He loves. [19]

My mind is set on the right, the lovely, the admirable: on all that is excellent and praiseworthy. I choose to think about these things. [20]

I have the mind of Christ. [21]

I am paying attention to the words the Lord is telling me by keeping them in my heart for they are Life and health to my whole body. Above all else, I am guarding my heart for it is the wellspring of my life. [22]

I have called on the Name of the Lord so there is deliverance for me. I am among the survivors and He has called me. [23]

I am close to the Lord for He is close to the brokenhearted and saves those crushed in spirit. I have been delivered out of ALL my troubles. [24]

I know that in all things God works for my good because I love Him and am called to accomplish His purposes. Therefore, God is for me and who can be against me? None! for Christ intercedes on my behalf. Who shall separate me from the love of Christ? Not trouble, hardship, persecution, famine, nakedness, danger, or the sword because I AM MORE THAN A CONQUEROR through Him who loves me. [25]

The Lord is my Shepherd so I will fear no evil when He prepares a table of blessing for me before my enemies! Goodness and love follow me all the days of my life and I choose to dwell in God's presence forever. [26]

For You are my hiding place; You will protect me from trouble and surround me with songs of deliverance. [27]

I submit myself to you, Father. I actively resist the Devil and all his hordes and he—even now—flees from me! [28]

Jesus Christ has given me authority to trample on snakes, scorpions, and to overcome all the power of the enemy. NOTHING WILL HARM ME. I do not rejoice only that the spirits must submit to me, but that my name is written in heaven. [29]

I intend to be strong in the Lord and in His mighty power. Therefore by an act of my will I put on the full armor of God so I can take my stand against the devil's schemes. For this reason, my struggle is not against flesh and blood but against all rulers, authorities, and powers of this dark world and against all the spiritual forces of evil in heavenly realms. I AM STANDING MY GROUND and when I am through with this battle on earth and everything else, I INTEND TO REMAIN STANDING...

Right now I am putting on the belt of truth, buckled around my waist; the breastplate of righteousness over my heart; my feet fitted out with the readiness that comes from having the Gospel of Peace within. In addition to all this, I take up the shield of faith with which I can extinguish ALL the flaming arrows of the evil one. I take my helmet of Salvation and the sword of the Spirit which is God's Word. I will pray in the Spirit on all occasions, keeping alert... [30]

For God has rescued me from this present evil age. [31]

I take the authority of the Christ within me and bind on earth all the powers and principalities of darkness, Satan, demons, devils, evil spirits, carnal spirits, curses, and occult forces in the Name of and by the Blood of Jesus Christ. Your promise is that those things are now bound in heaven. Likewise, I now take authority to loose the power of the Holy Spirit in me and over my family, loosing everything that Satan had bound so I may live in the very blessings of my Father. Be done now, in Jesus' Name. [32]

I acknowledge and confess that I am from God and have overcome every spirit that denies Christ has come in the flesh. I have overcome the spirit of Anti-christ because the One who is in me is far greater than the one who is in the world. [33]

I confess by an act of my will that I am born of God and will not continue to sin because God keeps me safe and the evil one cannot harm me. Even if the whole world is under the control of the evil one, Jesus Christ is True God and Eternal Life and will return for me at the appointed time. [34]

As acts of the Renewed Mind within me, I WILL to be joyful always, to pray continually, and to give thanks in all circumstances for I know this is God's will for me. I choose not to put out the Spirit's fire or to treat prophecies with contempt. I will test everything; hold on to the good and avoid every kind of evil so that the God of peace may sanctify me through and through in my whole spirit, soul, and body to be kept blameless until Christ's return. [35]

And just as I have received Christ Jesus as Savior, Deliverer, Healer, and Friend, I will continue to live in Him, rooted to the depths of my being and built to the heights of my potential. [36]

O Lord, confident that You have shown me a most excellent way to behave, I embrace LOVE. [37]

I actively pluck the fruit of the Holy Spirit so that the very character of God may be grown in my innerman. I appropriate Love as Joy, Peace, Patience, Kindness, Goodness, Faithfulness, Gentleness, and Self-control, choosing to live by the Spirit and keep in step with Him. [38]

I will bear fruit in every good work. [39]

By an act of my will I am rejoicing now and will rejoice in all things. I want my gentleness to be evident to all because the Lord is near. I WILL NOT TO BE anxious about anything but in everything by prayer and petition, with thanksgiving, present my requests to God. By this means the peace of God will transcend my human understanding and will guard my spirit and mind in Christ Jesus. [40]

Thank you, my precious heavenly Father, that I am a chosen person, a holy nation, a person belonging to You so that I might declare the praises of Christ who called me out of darkness into His wonderful light. [41]

My hope IS God, that in that day You will spread your tent over me and never again will I hunger. Never again will I thirst. The sun will not beat upon me nor any scorching heat for the Lamb at the center of the throne will be my Shepherd and You will lead me to springs of living water; and God will wipe away every tear from my eyes...

AMEN, PRAISE AND GLORY AND WISDOM AND THANKS AND HONOR AND POWER AND STRENGTH BE TO OUR GOD FOREVER AND EVER. AMEN AND AGAIN I SAY AMEN! [42]

APPENDIX II
Scriptural Key to the Confession of Victory

The Confession of Salvation

[1] Revelation 4:8
[2] Revelation 4:11
[3] Revelation 5:12
[4] I John 5:1-6
[5] Romans 3:22-25
[6] Romans 8:1-2
[7] I John 1:9
[8] John 6:63-65
[9] Colossians 3:10

The Confession of Water Baptism

[10] I John 5:7-12
[11] Acts 10:47

The Confession of Spirit Baptism

[12] John 7:37-39
[13] Matthew 3:11

The Confession of Assurance of Salvation

[14] Psalm 138:8-139:1-5
[15] Romans 8:16-17
[16] Phillipians 4:13
[17] Colossians 1:9-11

The Confession of Deliverance, Healing and Health

[18] Romans 12:1-2
[19] Colossians 1:13
[20] Philippians 4:7-8
[21] I Corinthians 2:16
[22] Proverbs 4:7-8
[23] Joel 2:32
[24] Psalm 34:16-17
[25] Romans 8:28-38
[26] Psalm 23
[27] Psalm 32:8

The Confession of Authority for Spiritual Warfare

[28] James 4:7
[29] Luke 10:19-20
[30] Ephesians 6:11-13
[31] Galatians 1:4

The Confession of Power to Bind Spirits

[32] Matthew 18:18
[33] I John 4:4

The Confession of Walking Worthy and in Blessing

[34] I John 5:18-20
[35] I Thessalonians 5:16-25
[36] Colossians 2:6-8

The Confession of Having the Fruit of the Spirit

[37] I Corinthians 12:31-13:13
[38] Galatians 5:22
[39] Colossians 1:10-11
[40] Philippians 4:4-7

The Confession of Thanksgiving and Praise

[41] I Peter 2:9-10
[42] Revelation 7:12

APPENDIX III
List of Occult Practices

To be free from the power of the occult, each and every known practice must be repented of and renounced individually, aloud. Begin by a sincere prayer for God's forgiveness for any and all involvement you have ever had with the occult. Next, renounce each one by reading them out loud as a testimony against Satan so he has no further legitimate right to vex you.

The list given here is not exhaustive. Should you know of any other occultic practices, literature you have read, groups, cults, or anything at all dealing in the occult that you have been involved in, add it for repentance and renunciation. Some things included here may be unfamiliar but go ahead and renounce them anyway as you read. Take your time with this list and be thorough. God bless you as you are freed of these chains.

A SIMPLE FORM FOR PRAYER IS: "LORD, IN THE NAME OF JESUS CHRIST I RENOUNCE_____
AND BIND SATAN'S POWER OVER ME."

RELIGIOUS ORGANIZATIONS AND FALSE CULTS

Bahai, Armstrongism, Unitarianism, The Way, Unity, Christian Science, Tao, Shintoism, Tai Chi, (all Eastern religions and mysticisms are devil-based), Rosicruscianism, Jehovah Witnesses, Buddhism in all forms, Yoga, Islam, Muslim doctrines, Zoroastrianism, Confucianism, Theosophical Society, Mormonism, Hara Krishna, Hinduism, Mohammedanism, Scientology (L. Ron Hubbard), Santeria, Sun Myung Moon, Divine Life Mission, The Love Family, secret societies of any kind, Eastern Star, Order of Masons (Freemasonry), Cabbalists, Mystery Religion/Teachings, Alchemists, Pyramidology, Worldwide Church of God, The Church Universal and Triumphant, The People's Temple, Alamo Christian Foundation, Unification Church, Spiritist Church, Church of Religious Science, Children of God, Human Potential Movement, Sufi Healing Order, Manifested Sons of God, Order of the Owl, Ouija Foundation, Church of Satan, Eckankar, Esoteric Brotherhoods of Mysticism, Occultism and magic, the National Council of Churches and the World Council of Churches.

ALL New Age religious organizations: Wicca, Mystery Babylon Religious System, New Group of World Servers, Tara Center, Planet

Stewards, Warriors of the Rainbow, Children of the Dawn, The Lucis Trust, Holistic Medicine, the Urantia Church, Institute for the Study of Conscious Evolution; The Planetary Commission for Global Healing and the Quartus Foundation for Spiritual Research (both headed by John Randolph Price), Lord Maitreya (New World "Messiah"), Mark Age, The Hierarchal Board, University of Life, The Plan, and all others.

OCCULT PHILOSOPHIES

Pantheism, Akikado, Pyramidology, Mind Sciences, Subud, Urantia, Metaphysics, Theosophy, Moral Rearmament, Religious Science, Spiritism, Scientology, Silva Mind Control, Holistic Movement, Mind Dynamics, Judo, Karate, Kung Fu, Taekwondo, New Age, Anhedonea, E.S.T. (Erhard Seminars), ECaP (B.S. Siegel), Lifespring, Sufism, PMA (Positive Mental Attitude), TM (Transcendental Meditation), Subliminal Mind Control (self-help "positive suggestion" tapes: even so-called "Christian" tapes).

Animism, ESP (Extrasensory Perception), Catistrophism, Ancient mythological societies (Baal, Ashtoreths, Teraphim, Egyptian, Greek, Roman, African, European, the Americas, and all Oriental and Eastern dieties); Karma, Reincarnation, I Am Self consciousness, Selfism (invoking the "self powers within" to become a god), Aquarianism, Anthrosophy, occultism, a prosperity gospel; GAIA (the planet "mother-earth" as a greater god to serve), Luciferism.

WITCHCRAFT, SATANISM, AND SPIRITISM

Numerology, Astrology, wishing well, consult or pray to the dead, sorcery, witchcraft, spiritism, black magic, white magic, Satan worship, Black Mass, curses, Grimoire (book of spells), and materialization. Omens, celebration of Halloween and any Satanist holiday, playing the Ouija game, spirit guides, American Indian (or other native) "guides", family ghosts, divination, Voodoo, Evil Eye, Tarot and Tarok Cards, palm or head readings, levitation, automatic writing, fortune telling, astral projection, horoscopes, horoscope readings from birthdate, The Root Man, consult a medium, attend or participate in a seance; tealeaf-, sand-, sticks-, stones-readings; use of a pendulum, love charms, crystals, or potions.

Chanting Eastern meditations, mantras, guided visualization, attempt to or practice of mental telepathy; use of divining rod, Indian rain dances, handwriting analyzed for the future, reading fortune cookies, a "magical" healing, occult games, hypnotized or have hypnotized others; psychedelic drugs; visit to false god temples or worship sites (even as a tourist), visiting Casadega, Florida, or other witch covens or spiritists' towns, homes, places of business; Stonehenge, Druidism; use of precognition or ESP, shamanism, viewing demonic movies, parapsychology, paranormal and poltergeist phenomena, necromancy, necrophilia, masquerades, psychokinesis, telekinesis (spoon bending), psychometry, clairvoyance, clairaudience, being or consulting a psychic, metapsychology, Discarnate Intelligence, attending seminars or public meetings of "guides".

Possession of occult symbols, masks, decorations: "good luck" charms, numbers or objects, rabbit's foot, Chinese Zodiac symbols, dragons, unicorns, peace symbols, upside-down cross, Satanic triangles, sun symbols, pentagrams, ALL prayer beads, worry stones, familiar objects; New Age symbols.

OCCULT LITERATURE

Jeanne Dixson's books and articles; Napoleon Hill's books,"Think and Grow Rich", "Success Through a Positive Mental Attitude", "The Magic Power of Belief"; Tolkein's "Ring Books"; "I Ching"; all Edgar Cayce materials; All Sybil Leek or other witch's literature; "Power of Positive Thought"; "Jonathan Livingston Seagull"; "Magic of Thinking Big"; "I Can"; all books by A. Ford, "Cybro-cybernetics"; "Love, Medicine & Miracles" (B.S. Siegel, MD); "Getting Well Again" (Simonton); "Dream Power" (Faraday). Any material by Anton LeVey including the "Satanic Bible".

PUBLISHERS: Anything at all published by these astrological and psychic printers: "Doorways To The Mind", "Fate", "Horoscope Guide", "Inner Light-Enlightment in the New Age", "Metapsychology-The Journal of Discarnate Intelligence", "New Realities", "Prediction-The Magazine for Astrology and the Occult", "The Unexplained-The Unknown Visited and Explained". Alice Bailey, Barry McWaters, John Randolph Price books.

The following are occultic books, comic books, TV cartoons, movies, and toys reaching our children as researched by Texe Marrs from his excellent book, "Dark Secrets of the New Age". All Texe Marrs' books are recommended for further enlightment. These occultic and New Age materials are found in school and public libraries or may be a part of some school curriculums.

BOOKS: "MACOS" (Man: A Course of Study) teaches children genocide, homosexuality, euthanasia; "The Dragons of North Chittendon (Susan Fromberg Schaeffer), "The Dragon ABC Hunt" for three to six year-olds (Loreen Leedy), "Secret Spells and Curious Charms" (Monika Beisner), "King Stork" (Howard Pyle), "I Will Call It Georgie's Blues" (Suzanne Newton), "Watermusic" (Sarah Sargent), "Nelson Malone Meets the Man from Mush-nut" (Louise Hawes), "Dragon Dance" (John Christopher), "Elliott and Win" (Carolyn Meyer). There are literally hundreds of these.

TELEVISION: "Thundercats" (full of sorcery images and the magical eye of Thundra (the Third Eye of Hindus and All-seeing eye of the Egyptian-Babylonian sun god, Horus); main character talks to his dead father's spirit, his magic sword levitates, Yoga exercises, serpents, demons gods portrayed. "The Smurfs" have New Age scriptwriters, directors, and producers show New Age occult symbolism, levitation, magical chants, Satanic pentagram. Papa Smurf uses enchantment to ward off evil. "Rainbow Brite" is the New Age's representation of man's bridge to godhood. "She-Ra, Princess of Power" is a fantasized story of MYSTERY BABYLON, MOTHER OF HARLOTS incarnate. "He-Man, Master of the Universe" is a supernatural man-god with occultic symbols and practices as pyramid and crystal power, serpents, the Satanic ram's head, skull, witches' charms and spells. Be on the lookout for more.

MOVIES: "E.T." and any other Spielberg productions that are occultic, "Close Encounters of the Third Kind", "Star Wars" Series, "Ninja" movies, "Dune" (young man's initiation into godhood), "Raiders of the Lost Ark" and "Temple of Doom" expose children to 'powers' and then how to enter into their exercise, "The Last Temptation of Christ", and others too numerous to mention.

TOYS: toys, dolls, and figurines of licensed cartoon characters such as She-Ra, He-man, Masters of the Universe, (Mattel) etc. Skeletor (look at instructions that come with it), Godbox (guarantees a direct line to God), Power Lords with "Shaya, Queen of Power" (extraterrestrial), "Raygoth", "Gapplog" and "Crystlar" which introduces children to a strange world where magic reigns following a cosmic demon war. Other toys include Dungeons and Dragons, Dragonraid, skateboards now being sold by Toys R Us with hideous dragons. Look for toys (and T-shirts) with small Satanic triangles, hexagrams, pentagrams, upside-down crosses, swastikas, lightning bolts, occultic symbols, 666.

There are many, many more materials. You will know which books, articles, or literature you have read that are occultic in nature. Also, ask the

Lord to reveal them to you. Even if you cannot remember the names of those publications, television presentations or movies, include them in your confession as all general occultic influences which you have ever attended, read, or come in contact with.

Be prepared to discover and renounce other occultic participations as an on-going cleansing of your life by the Lord as new things are revealed. It is plain to see that deliverance is the constant application of the cross-life in self-denial along with reliance on the Lord to meet all spiritual needs. It is not easy. It may not be a quick work in your life. But allow the cleansing to continue by obedience and laying down of those evil things which the Lord desires to liberate you from.

APPENDIX IV
Glossary of Terms

Abortion—The willful taking of a human life in utero during the nine-month period of pregnancy. It is a human life sacrifice to the devil before the idol of "self". God is the Master of Life which is extremely sacred. Miscarriages are natural: God-allowed expulsions are not to be confused with willful, malicious abortion (Psalm 139:13-16).

Absalom Spirit—Conspiracy to steal royal or governmental power and authority by malcontented deceit; usually from an insider position (Absalom, King David's son—2 Samuel 15).

Abyss—Conceived of as the subterranean abode of demonic hordes (Rev 20:1; Lk 8:31). The Greek word means "very deep" or "bottomless" and is used in the Septuagent (Greek translation of the Old Testament) to translate the Hebrew word for the primeval deep (Ge 1:2, 7:11; Pr 8:28). It is a place set apart by God for the confinement of Satan and evil spirits.

Aesculapius—The Greco-Roman god of medicine. It has been a symbol of medicine for hundreds of centuries.

Ahriman—A hostile spirit: Ahura Mazda's antagonist who is a spirit of darkness and evil in Zoroastrianism.

Amulet—An ornament or charm supposedly charged with magical powers and used to ward off spells, disease and bad luck.

Ancient One—A name sometimes given to an officiating priestess at a Black Satanic Mass.

Arcana—A secret process or formula; in Tarot, 22 pictorial cards make up the major Arcan and 56 (or 52) cards divided into four suits are the minor Arcana. See Tarot and Tarok.

Artemis—Greek for Roman goddess Diana-Cybele, the mother goddess of fertility worshipped in Asia Minor; "many-breasted, fallen from heaven" (Acts 19:24-25, an Ephesian diety).

Ashtoreth—Goddess of love, fertility and war. Often paired with a male diety like Baal. Female dieties such as Astoreth (consort of Baal) and Asherah (consort of EL, the chief god of the Canaanite pantheon). Ashtoreth was associated with the evening star and was the beautiful goddess of war and fertility. She was worshipped as Ishtar in Babylonia and as Ashtart in Aram. To the Greeks she was Astarte or Aphrodite, and to the Romans, Venus. Worship of the Ashtoreths involved extremely lascivious practices (1 Ki 14:24; 2 Ki 23:7). See Baal and Six-Six-Six.

Astral Projection—Symbolized by a witch on a broom; the demonic empowering through a person's spirit to project his or her soul away and apart from their body (out-of-body experiences) to another location where they can see, hear, touch, smell. It is ungodly and a part of the fallen nature that is used by Satan.

Appendix IV

Augury—The divination from omens or portents predicting things to come to pass from chance events as the fall of lots or dice.

Baal—A word meaning "lord". Baal, the god worshiped by the Canaanites and Phoenicians, was variously known to them as the son of Dagon and the son of El. In Aram (Syria), he was called Hadad and in Babylonia, Adad. Believed to give fertility to the womb and life-giving rain to the soil, he is pictured as standing on a bull, popular symbol of fertility and strength (1 Ki 12:28). The storm cloud was his chariot, thunder his voice, and lightning his spear and arrows. The worship of Baal involved sacred prostitution and sometimes child sacrifice (Jer 19:5).

Bacchus—The Greek god of wine (Dionysus); excess revelry, orgies, glorification of drunkenness, the "party spirit".

Baculum—A witch's wand, staff or broomstick.

Balaam Spirit—Balaam was a corrupt teacher who deceived God's people into compromise with worldliness. Balaam advised the Midianite women how to lead the Israelites away from God (Numbers 25:1-2, 31:16, Jude 11).

Black Magic—Magic used for harm, deceit or destruction; satanist's rites and incantations used to curse.

Black Mass—A travesty of the Christian mass (the Eucharist or Lord's supper) by which satanists blaspheme God and ridicule Christianity; possible human sacrifice, the drinking of human or animal blood and other abominable practices.

Blessing—The favor of God, fruitfulness, prosperity, right relationship with God. Only God blesses: Satan and his agents cannot bless. Humans can bring and be a blessing to themselves, to other human beings, to creation, and to God. See Chapter 6.

Cantrip—A spell cast by a witch; a witch's "trick" against others.

Channeling—A New Age term for demon possession where a consenting human allows his or her own spirit and voice be the "channel" for an evil spirit's manifestation. Some channelers have familiar spirits with names like Lazaris, Seth, Saint Germain, Mafu, "Jesus", Abraham Lincoln, or Ramtha; they charge fees to allow the spirits to make appearances or teachings and are used as a mouthpiece for New Age literature coming straight from the mind of Satan in the form of "bibles" and "prophecies". This is an international phenomena and popular with some movie stars and world leaders.

Charm—Chanted or spoken words used to invoke a spell; also an object said to have supernatural power.

Clairaudience—The power or faculty of hearing something not present to the ear but regarded as having objective reality.

Clairvoyant—A person who uses clairvoyance which is the power or faculty of discerning objects not present to the senses; ability to perceive matters beyond the range of ordinary perception.

Coven—A group of satanists or witches, usually numbering not more than 13 (six males, six females, one leader), which meets regularly to worship Satan and work spells.

Curse—A charm or spell designed to cause harm or be destructive cast by Satan's representatives (witches, in rock music, etc.), by humans, God's agents, and prophets. God Himself can bring curses upon people in certain circumstances (1 Sa 19:9).

Diotrephes Spirit—Arrogant, dictatorial spirit of a church leader who gossips and puts brothers out of the fellowship one way or another; division of the sheep from leadership (3 John 9).

Demons or Devils—To occultists—any non-human spirit. According to the Word of God, an angel who rebelled against God, fell from heaven and now roams the earth seeking entrance in or against humans, animals, or objects in order to molest, vex, harrass, and encourage breaches between humankind and God. Such demons could cause mental disorder (Jn 10:20), violent actions (Lk 8:26), bodily disease (Lk 13:11,16), and rebellion against God (Rev 16:14). Their purpose is to kill and take people into Hell with them as they obey their lord and master, Satan.

Divination—The art or practice that seeks to foresee or foretell future events or discover hidden knowledge gained by the interpretation of omens or by the aid of supernatural powers. Corruption of the word divine, meaning God-like.

Divining Rod—A forked rod or stick believed to indicate the presence of water or minerals by dipping downward when held over a natural vein as a result of "spiritual", occultic means.

Dragons—Dragons abound in the mythology of ancient peoples (Liviathan in Canaanite lore, Set-Typhon, the red crocodile of Egypt). Metaphorically used to depict the enemies of God and of Israel (Re 12:3, Ps 74:14, Ez 29:3).

Eckankar—An organization teaching that man can only reach an advanced spiritual state by communicating with "spiritual travelers" and other "highly developed persons in the other worlds" (actual demons); there is use of soul travel and out-of-body experiences in this religion.

Familiar Spirits—A demonic spirit who serves a witch or medium, or who inhabits animals; appears at seances and may act as an impersonating agent; a demon who is "familiar" with the witch it works with in carrying out tasks for the witch or Satan.

Gargoyles—A hideous figure of a grotesque human or animal form used as practical or decorative features on buildings or furniture thought by pagans to ward off evil spirits.

Gnome—An ageless, often deformed "fanciful" dwarf who lives in the earth and guards precious, unmined ore or treasures; an elemental being in the theory of Paracelsus (1493-1541 AD) that inhabits the earth. Popular figure used in fairy tales.

Gnostics—False prophets speaking under the influence of spirits alienated from God must be tested (1 Jn 4:1-4). One of the most dangerous heresies of the first two centuries and rampant today, it teaches that the (human) spirit is entirely good and matter (body) is entirely evil; salvation is the escape from the body achieved not by faith in Christ but by special knowledge. An ascetic and licentious religion.

God—In Hebrew, is one God in three parts: God the Father, God the Son-Jesus Christ, and God the Holy Spirit. His power is over all. He is Lord of lords, King of all kings. These names reveal Who He is for His children: 1) JEHOVAH-TSIDKENU, "Jehovah Our Righteousness"; 2) JEHOVAH-M'KADDESH, "Jehovah Who Sanctifies" (and keeps); 3) JEHOVAH-SHALOM, "Jehovah Is Peace"; 4) JEHOVAH-SHAMMAH, "Jehovah Is There" (ever-flowing, present One); JEHOVAH-ROPHE, "Jehovah Heals" (and delivers); 5) JEHOVAH-JIREH, "Jehovah's Provision Shall Be Seen"; 6) JEHOVAH-NISSI, "Jehovah My Banner" (for battle); 7) JEHOVAH-ROHI, "Jehovah My Shepherd".

Grimoire—A book of spells that belongs to an individual or coven.

Holy Bible—The inerrant Word of God consisting of both the Old and New Testaments; to be believed, relied upon, and afforded a place of sacred respect in its often use. Jesus Christ stated, *"Blessed is he who keeps the words of the prophecy of this book"* and, *"I warn everyone who hears the words of the prophecy of this book: if anyone adds anything to them, God will add to him the plagues described in this book. And if anyone takes words away from this book of prophecy, God will take away from him his share in the tree of life and in the holy city, which are described in this book"* (Re 22:7, 18-19). All other bibles are false.

Jesus Christ—The ONLY Christ, only begotten Son of the Father, Jehovah-God and part of the Holy Trinity of Father, Son and Holy Spirit. He is divine God. He was conceived by the power of the Holy Spirit and became incarnate (a human being) from the Virgin Mary (a human, Jewish mother who was not and is not divine). He lived on the earth about 33 years and was at all times obedient to the Father. He suffered physical death on Calvary's Cross which was His perfect offering to God on behalf of all humanity's penalty of their sin nature, thus freeing humankind from the power of sin and death. He ascended from the grave in resurrection power, opening the way for eternal life to those who receive Him and live for Him as their only Lord and Savior, enduring to the end. He is returning for His own at the appointed-of-God time in an open show of victory over all principalities, powers, kingdoms, and world systems. He is alive now and presently seated at the right hand of God the Father, interceeding for the saints. There is no other way of salvation except through personal faith in Jesus Christ as Savior.

Jezebel Spirit— Wresting the authority of a headship and using for self purposes. In the church, one (male or female) who seduces or manipulates a ministry away from the recognized head.

Lady—To satanists, the female leader of a coven.

Libertine Spirit—Partying, orgies, drunkenness, licentiousness, "anything goes", sexual immorality, envy, argumentativeness, selfish ambitions, fits of rage, dissensions; vices which gratify the flesh—either mentally in libertine philosophies—or in the body to bring pleasure (Ga 5:16-21).

Legion—A Roman legion was made up of 6,000 men. In Mark 5:9, the term suggests possession with many powers opposed to Jesus and/or numerous demons residing within one person.

Levitation—The act or process of levitating by means held supernatural; to rise or float in the air in defiance of gravitation, usually done during a spiritualistic seance.

Ligature—A spell (curse) which prevents a person from doing something cast onto them by a witch, warlock, or coven.

Lycanthropy—(Wer-man, Wolf-animal): werewolf; a belief that one has taken on a wolf appearance (or possibly another wer-animal) by the use of witchcraft or demonic magic in order to bring physical harm.

Magic— Its root words are Magos and Magus meaning "sorcerer" (of Iranian origin). Used in the occult to influence and control people; the use of means (as charms, spells, curses) believed to have supernatural powers over natural forces; extraordinary negative influence to bewitch and control; tricks of illusion and sleight of hand; enchantment.

Magister—The male leader of a coven.

Magis—A male witch, sorcerer; conjurer who practices magic arts: wizard. One that performs feats of sleight of hand and illusion, magician, juggler (originally).

Materialization—The physical manifestation of a spirit being; to cause to appear from the dead; to put in an appearance from spirit to material form: a vision, apparition, ghost.

Mantis—Greek root word meaning "diviner, prophet"; akin to be mad or manic; relating to the faculty of divination.

Mantra—"Sacred" counsel and formula from the mind: a mystical form for invocation or incantation (as in Hinduism and TM). A mantra is a personalized word-chant (each devotee has his or her own) and is used to put the mind into a blank state for receiving "wisdom". It is an unholy, mystical word(s) to invoke demon spirit guides to come. False prophets have used even Christian choruses repeatedly in a service to induce a trance-like state as a way to get people "in the spirit" (very common with snake handling religions). God never calls to blank out the mind or lose control of it: acceptable worship to Him is to worship in truth with the whole spirit, soul and mind, voluntarily and in love.

Mask—Masque, maschera, "to cover or partially cover the face used for disguise". A figure of a head worn or a grostesquely carved head or face used as an ornament; keystone; something that serves to conceal or disguise: pretense, cloak; to take part in a masquerade; to cover over, as sin.

Masochism—Sexual perversion of gaining pleasure in being abused or dominated by the love object.

Meditation—Godly use of meditation is a Christian's active, self-controlled, and conscious prayer and adoration going God-ward from the spirit: it is not a trance state (passive mind). Ungodly meditation comes from the relinquishing of a passive mind over to another entity (demonic) which is usually based on the Hindu principle of linking the human mind with the Universal Mind. Common to all eastern religions and taught in psychology as a way to "draw on hidden powers from within".

Necromancy—To pray to or attempt to conjure up the spirit(s) of the dead for purposes of magically revealing the future or influencing the course of events; sorcery. Deceived people through seances, visualization, Yoga exercises or meditation are attempting to contact relatives, famous figures and even "Jesus". Demons will answer to those names because they are lying spirits, posing as anyone to gain entrance.

Necrophilia—Obsession with an unusually erotic interest in or stimulation by corpses, the dead, murder or death.

New Age Movement—Religion having four basic tenets: 1) God is all; all is God (all true reality is divine), 2) Personal enlightenment is necessary since all people live in ignorance of their "divine" nature, 3) All enlightenment comes from the spirit world, altered states of consciousness and psychic powers, and 4) A united world is the solution to human problems by social, economic, religious, and political means. New Agers are dedicated to preparing their followers for a perfect "heaven on earth" and use occultic means to achieve it.

New Age Symbols—Pentagram (five-pointed star), Enneagram (nine points within a circle), the shapes of triangles, diamonds circles, crescent moons, swastikas, and the hexagram. Other belief tenets are symbolized by suns, rainbows, the lotus, crystals, dragons and serpents, the yin/yang, unicorns, the pegasus (flying horse), centaurs, mermaids, 666, the all-seeing eye, Egyptian ankh, Star of David (corrupted and often mixed with other symbols); by wheels, the mandala circle for Satan, and by the karmic wheel representing birth, death, then reincarnation.

Number Of The Beast—"6-6-6" is man's number (Rev 13:18); also the number taken by adherents of New Age philosphy from ancient Babylonia as the triple Aphrodite.

Numerology—The occult study of the significance of numbers in a person's life, to a nation, or any other object in question with each number having a "certain power" relating to an occultic connection.

Occult—From the Latin "occultus" meaning secret or hidden, to conceal; from hell: not revealed or easily detected or apprehended. The occult refers to secret or hidden knowledge available to satanist initiates; is hidden knowledge of the supernatural and deals in parapsychology and paranormal phenomena. It involves the action or influence of (evil) supernatural agencies or some secret knowledge about them and is as old as Satan's activity on earth to produce his kingdom.

Omen—A prophetic sign; an occurrence or phenomenon believed to portend a future event: augury.

Parapsychology—Study concerned with the investigation of evidence for telepathy, clairvoyance and psychokinesis.

Pergamum—Modern Pergama, Turkey. The ancient capital of Asia, built on a cone-shaped hill rising 1,000 feet above the surrounding valley. Its name in Greek means "citadel" and is the origin of our word "parchment." Satan ruled from Pergamum when it was the official center of emperor worship in Asia (Re 2:12-13). Satan rules as the Principality over the center of man's world power.

Philistine Spirit—Continual struggle for permanent control of the land and possessions that God has reserved for His children. Spiritual philistines are uncircumcised: they will not be brought under God's authority. Philistines produce Goliaths: God produces Davids.

Poltergeist—Greek "poltern" to knock, and "geist" spirit or ghost. A noisy "mischievous" ghost held to be responsible for unexplained noises, tappings, footfalls, or knocks.

Precognition—To know an event beforehand; clairvoyance relating to an event or state not yet experienced. A feeling, dream, or visualization that something is going to happen and it comes to pass. Precognition is Satan's counterfeit of the gift of the Word of Knowledge or a prophetic word from the Lord.

Psychic—A medium, witch, magus. Greek root "psyche" soul. Knowledge lying outside the sphere of physical science: immaterial, moral or spiritual in orgin or force. A person who is sensitive to nonphysical or supernatural forces of influence; a person operating under demonic influence out of their soul-state.

Psychology—The pseudoscience of the mind and study of human behavior. It involves itself with manipulating the mind, will, intellect and emotions (soul) in proscribed manners of treatment. Psychology is worldly-wisdom that attempts to heal and fix the soul without bringing it into proper submission to the Spirit of God. Christians direct themselves to Jesus Christ to solve their human problems out of a renewed and re-born spirit.

Psychokinesis—Movement of physical objects by the mind without use of physical means; may be used in conjunction with precognition and telekinesis.

Psychometry—Divination of facts concerning an object or its owner through contact with, or proximity to, the object. Used by some police investigators through mediums' occultic skills.

Sabbat—A quarterly or semi-quarterly meeting of witches or satanists.

Sadism—Delight in cruelty; sexual perversion of bringing mental and/or physical pain to the love object.

Satan—Hebrew word is "Satan" translated directly. Revelation 20:1-3 reveals other names for him as "the dragon", "that ancient serpent", "the devil", "the Accuser", Lucifer; others include Shiva, Satanas, Sanat. Satan is the archenemy of God, God's nation Israel, and enemy of all Christians. Michael, an archangel of God and protector of Israel, defeated Satan in heavenly warfare in Daniel 12:1. Satan is given limited power by God to afflict evil on men or against nature and is under God's full control (Job 1:8-19, Heb 2:14). Christians are given authority from Christ to resist and cast Satan out as overcomers.

Satyr—Hebrew root word for Satan; it is depicted as lower half goat, upper half man with horns. Later, it was a Sylvan diety of Greek mythology fond of revelry with lecherous, abnormal male sexual cravings. It is a New Age symbol for Satan depicted by a goat's head in an inverted pentagram or cicle.

Seal—The demon's summoning signature or diagram.

SIX-SIX-SIX (666)—The number of the Beast and identifying mark of the Antichrist and his followers. Can be traced to the ancient Babylonian religion which primarily worshipped a Mother Goddess (The Queen of Heaven of Rev 17). Satan's last days' revival of Babylonianism includes SIX as a number symbolizing the sacramental sexual ecstasy in which the worshippers achieve union with the divine universe and with the Queen of Heaven (Ashtoreth, Anath, Asherah, the Great Whore, Babylon the Great, the Mother of Harlots); 666 is a Satanic 'holy' number, representing the "Triple Aphrodite" of her unholy trinity as Mother-Father-Son. The number 69 (one upright 6, one unside-down six) is another obscene sexual symbol.

Spiritist—A male or female medium. Consulting a medium is the same as being one (De 18:10-11). Death by stoning was God's sentence against all mediums (Lev 20:21).

Sorcery—Magic, usually of the black variety; behaving as a witch, sorcerer or sorceress; the use of power gained from the assistance or control of evil spirits, especially for divining.

Subliminal Mind Control—Latin for "below the threshold"; to produce a sensation or a perception existing or functioning outside the area of conscious awareness; to divert the conscious in another direction by a power outside the mind in order to control its thought patterns. This method is not to be used by Christians in any guise.

Tarok—An ancient card game popular in Central Europe and played with a pack containing 40, 52 (standard modern deck), or 56 cards equivalent to present day playing cards plus the 22 Tarot cards used as trump cards.

Tarot Cards—Fortune telling cards used by spiritists made up of a deck of 22 pictorial cards, each card representing certain portents or "fortunes".

Telekinesis—The apparent production of motion in objects (as by a spiritualistic medium) without contact or other physical means; spoon bending, etc.

Teraphim—Household gods; portable idols representing a desired trait like safety or protection (Ge 31:19). May be lifesized and resemble humans (1 Sa 19:13-17). Teraphim were consulted (prayed or spoken to) in Eze 21:21. Demons inhabit the object and enslave the owner by dependence on belief of the object. A modern-day teraphim may be a small statue of "St. Christopher", believed to keep people safe while in travel.

Unicorn—A mythological (from ancient Babylonian love feasts), one-horned animal generally depicted with the body and head of a horse, the hind legs of a stag, the tail of a lion, and a single horn in the middle of the forehead; it is tamed by virgins.

Unicorn—A mythological (from ancient Babylonian love feasts), one-horned animal generally depicted with the body and head of a horse, the hind legs of a stag, the tail of a lion, and a single horn in the middle of the forehead; it is tamed by virgins.

Unisex Bible—Promoted by the National Council of Churches, liberal churchmen, New Age leaders, and radical feminist groups demanding the words "Lord" and "King" be replaced by "Sovereign"; also the word "God" to be changed to "Our Father and Mother", "Son" (Jesus the Christ) be replaced with "child", and "she" and "her" to refer to God. These changes will, at the least, sow Scriptural confusion, discord and heresy in the Church and will correlate with the Mystery Religious system of Babylon.

Upside-Down Cross—Often used as a mockery of the cross of Christ; sometimes shown with the "arms" broken (peace symbol). Another cross satanists incorporate is an upside-down question mark-cross, questioning the deity of Jesus; Hitler's swastikas.

Visualization— To conjure up an image of a spirit he or she wishes to contact (a relative or famous person like George Washington, Socrates, etc.). Guided visualization is used in modern psychology and in cultic churches wherein a leader gifted in this technique helps set the scene by having the patient or group blank out their minds and imagine exactly what they are being told. A candle flame, crystal, or mandala is often used to focus one's eyes on as they listen. Demonic spirits may or may not appear.

Voodoo—Of African origin "tutelary diety, demon". An occultic religion derived from African ancestor worship practiced chiefly by Haitians, characterized by propitiatory rites and communication by trance with animistic deities. One who deals in spells and necromancy; a sorcerer's spell. Voodoo hex: a hexed object that is charmed. It combines magic, spiritism, death curses and the use of fetishes to intimidate, harm or kill the person of its object.

Warlock— One that breaks faith (troth) with the Devil; to lie. A man practicing the black arts; sorcerer, conjurer.

Weird—Of or relating to or caused by witchcraft or the supernatural: magical, odd, fantastic, eerie, uncanny; ill fortune, fate, destiny, of a soothsayer. "Weird Sisters" were the fates of mythology carried forth in British myth.

White Magic—So called "good magic" supposedly beneficial practiced by witches. No curse can bless.

Witch—Female medium who practices magic although some witches prefer to practice either white or black magic. Biblically, a spiritist to contact the dead (1 Sa 28:7-20).

Wolf Spirit—Those already in or wanting to come into the church who appear as believers but are there to maim sheep, ravage the flock of God, and destroy the work of God in a fellowship (Mk 7:15, Jn 10:12); undermines the shepherd to split a church and steal sheep (Ac 20:28-31).

Worldly Wisdom Spirit—It is recognized in people who feel they have the answers for life apart from using God's heavenly wisdom. It comes from advice columnists, self-help "pop psychology" books, articles and "experts" over television and radio programs. It is earthly, unspiritual, soulish and of the devil, and does not bring peace (Ja 3:13-18) because it deals with stirring up the soul.

Yoga— A Hindu theistic philosophy teaching the suppression of all activity of body, mind, and will in order that the "self" may realize its distinction from them and attain liberation; a system of exercises for attaining bodily or mental control with direct linkage to demonic powers.

Yogi—An adherent who practices yoga; a markedly reflective or mystical person who leads others into error; spirit guides.

Zodiac—An imaginary belt in the heavens 18 degrees wide that encompasses the apparent paths of all the principal planets except Pluto and has the ecliptic as its central line. It is divided into 12 constellations or signs, each taken for astrological purposes to extend 30 degrees of longitude. So-called signs of the heavens in the Zodiac are Aris (ram), Taurus (bull), Gemini (twins), Cancer (crab), Leo (lion), Virgo (virgin), Libra (balance), Scorpio (scorpion), Sagittarius (archer), Capricorn (goat), Aquarius (water bearer), Pisces (fishes). Spiritualists use these signs in astrology to project divination and influences (supposedly from the stars and planets) onto human affairs and terrestrial events. This is inspired of Hell and also a way for some to make money on unsuspecting and gullible fools. It is strickly forbidden to the Christian.

Zombie—(Niger-Congo origen; akin to the Kongo Nzambi god). The voodoo snake diety; the supernatural power that according to voodoo belief, may enter into and reanimate a dead body; a will-less and speechless human in the West Indies capable only of automatic movement who is held to have died and been reanimated but often believed to have been drugged into a catalepsy for the hours of interment. It is part of the cult "Zombi".

APPENDIX V
Occult Holidays

Satan continues in his attempts to pervert and convert the natural and God-ordered creation to serve his ends. He is the supreme counterfeiter of all that is true, striving to garner as much honor, attention and adulation as possible in competing with Jesus Christ. For this reason he has given his children (satanists and pagans) their own days of celebration in pale image of Christian days of worship.

There are four major holidays that come from religions in which the moon or a moon goddess is worshiped as a major deity. Halloween, Candlemas, Beltane and Lammas fall in this category. CHRISTIANS AND THEIR CHILDREN SHOULD HAVE NOTHING TO DO WITH THESE UNHOLY AND DEMONIC HOLIDAYS. We are to avoid all appearance of evil, keeping ourselves unspotted from the world system which is Satan's kingdom.

The other four lesser occultic holidays of Yule, Vernal Equinox, Saint John's Eve and Michaelmas are based on the natural solstices and equinoxes. Soltices are the natural events of longest and shortest days of the year. Equinoxes are the days in which night and day are the same length.

1. HALLOWEEN—October 31. Halloween is the end and beginning of the witches' year. It marks the beginning of the death and destruction associated with winter. At this time, the power of the underworld is unleashed and spirits are supposedly freed to roam about the earth. Occultists consider Halloween the best time to contact spirits. (So, Christian, why would you want your children or grandchildren out roaming around on Halloween for a handful of candy?) The closest Christian festival is the next day, November 1, Hallowmas or, "All Saints Day".

2. CANDLEMAS—February 2. Historically by satanists, Candlemas was a celebration of lengthening days and the approach of spring. In Christianity, it is observed as a church festival in commemoration of the presentation of Christ in the temple and the Hebrew purification of the Virgin Mary.

3. BELTANE—April 30 (Also Walpurgis Night). Beltane roughly coincides with the time for planting crops. The Celts and some others offered human sacrifices at this time. Walpurgis Night is an occultic event witches ride to at an appointed rendezvous, having a nightmarish quality. The closest Christian tradition (from A.D. 777), is in celebration of a saint whose feast day falls on May 1st.

4. LAMMAS—July 31. Lammas occurs about the time when fruits and vegetables are ripening and the harvest season is beginning. On the next day, August 1, Christians brought loaves of bread from the first ripe grain offering it to the church for consecration.

5. YULE—December 22. The winter solstice, or shortest day of the year marks a special event for celebration to satanists. In Christianity, December 24th is the nativity (human birth) of Jesus Christ and December 25th (Christmas Day) is set aside for the united celebration of Christ's birth through church services (mass) with the Eucharist.

6. VERNAL EQUINOX—March 21. Day and night are the same length, with days getting longer.

7. SAINT JOHN'S EVE—June 22, Midsummer. The summer solstice, or longest day of the year.

8. MICHAELMAS—September 22. The autumnal equinox when day and night are the same length and the days getting shorter. In Christianity, the nearest feast day is September 29th as a celebration to remember Saint Michael the Archangel who traditionally fought on behalf of Israel, God's chosen people.

APPENDIX VI
Bibliography

The Amplified Bible, (Grand Rapids, MI: The Zondervan Corp.).

The Holy Bible, King James Version, (New York: The World Publishing Company).

Kenneth Barker, *The New International Version Study Bible,* (Grand Rapids, MI: The Zondervan Corp), 1985.

Dietrich Bonhoeffer, *The Cost of Discipleship,* (New York: Collier Books, MacMillan Publishing Co.), 1961.

Fact Sheet On Satanism, Focus on the Family, (Mike Warnke Ministries, P.O. Box 472, Burgin, KY 40310), 1988.

Texe Marrs, *Dark Secrets of the New Age,* (Westchester, IL: Crossway Books, Good News Publishers), 7th Ed., 1987.

Texe Marrs, *Mystery Mark of the New Age,* (Westchester, IL: Crossway Books, Good News Publishers), 1988.

Jesse Penn-Lewis, *Soul and Spirit,* (South Molton-Devon, Great Britain: Overcomer Publications, Gospel Press).

Derek Prince, *From Curse to Blessing,* (Derek Prince Ministries, P.O. Box 300, Ft. Lauderdale, FL 33302), 1986.

Clair Ries, *Do Your Lions Have Lockjaw?,* 9 ed. unpublished, (P.O. Box 360396, Melbourne, Florida: World Missionary Fellowship, Inc.), 1986.

James Strong, *Strong's Exhaustive Concordance of the Bible* (Nashville, TN: Abingdon Publishers), 1977.

Daniel Webster, *Webster's New Collegiate Dictionary,* 150th ed., (Springfield, MASS: G. & C. Merriam Company), 1981.